THE TRUE PRINCIPLES

AND

AN APOLOGY

THE TRUE PRINCIPLES

OF

Pointed or Christian Architecture

AND

AN APOLOGY

FOR

The Revival of Christian Architecture

AUGUSTUS WELBY PUGIN

with an Introduction by
RODERICK O'DONNELL

True Principles first published in 1841 by John Weale, London
An Apology first published in 1843 by John Weale, London

This joint edition published in 2003

Gracewing
2 Southern Avenue, Leominster
Herefordshire HR6 0QF

ISBN 0 85244 611 X

Additional typesetting by
Action Publishing Technology Ltd
Gloucester GL1 5SR

Printed in England by
Antony Rowe Ltd
Eastbourne BN23 6QT

THIS VOLUME IS
DEDICATED TO THE INSPIRATION
OF
CLIVE WAINWRIGHT
1942–1999

INTRODUCTION

My writings much more than what I have been able to do have revolusionised the Taste of England

A.W.N. Pugin to John Hardman, *c.*1851

Augustus Welby Pugin's own assessment of the relative importance of his writings and his buildings, made to his great friend John Hardman towards the end of his short life (1812–1852), and even shorter career as a practicing architect, strikes us as a rather melancholy one. Yet most mid-Victorian commentators would have agreed with him.

In an age of booming opportunities in print, Pugin's books, pamphlets and journalism established him as an architectural and Catholic controversialist; although long in their influence his books were short-lived as publications. These had begun with his *Contrasts, or, A parallel between the noble edifices of the fourteenth and fifteenth centuries and similar buildings of the present day: Shewing the present decay of taste*; the first edition (1836) made Pugin a marked man amongst Protestants, while the second edition (1841) alienated a number of Catholics. The plates of *Contrasts* were more important than the text: Pugin drew and etched all his own plates, and it is the *contrasted* illustrations, which make *Contrasts* live. He was a brilliant draughtsman, with a very wide knowledge of English and Continental medieval architecture; he been trained in his father's drawing office and had measured and drawn many monuments for the publication *Examples of Gothic Architecture* (1831–8). The name Pugin would have been well known in the world of architectural practice from this title, but *Contrasts* must have seemed the work of an *enfant terrible*. Certainly no architectural publisher would handle it and so it had to be published privately, from Pugin's own new-built Gothic house, St Marie's Grange, Salisbury. The Catholic Charles Dolman published the second edition (1841).

Before 1836 Pugin had been drawing architectural 'contrasts' (curiously anticipating the modern art historical 'compare and contrast' method of studying pairs of images). This visual narrative-polemical method was not new, drawing on the long tradition of Antiquarian lamentation on the destruction of the past. Its object was to lambaste the Anglican Establishment which at best he tolerated for its role of occupying the desiccated husks of the great medieval Catholic *Ecclesia Anglicana*. On the architectural evidence alone, Pugin allows for no 'via media', and current scholarship on the sixteenth-century Reformation (Eamon Duffy, *The Stripping of the Altars* (1992) and *The Voices of Morebath*

(2001) largely agrees with him). Like much of his subsequent journalism, Pugin also intended to shock Catholics out of their chapel-building habits and to render certain existing Catholic architects unemployable. In the case of Charles Day, architect of the new neoclassical churches at Hereford and Bury St Edmund's (the latter is described by Pugin as 'a semi-pagan abortion'), this is just what happened.

Pugin's trenchant social and religious criticism of what were to be the 'hungry forties' was part romantic, part historical, and shared much with many other authors and critics of the received views of the Reformation and of contemporary social issues, such as the radical William Cobbet, the Whig Thomas Carlyle, the Catholic Romantic Kenelm Digby, and the young novelist and politician Benjamin Disraeli. Pugin was also aware of French Catholic Revival writers such as de Montalembert, de Lamennais and A. F. Rio, and it is their *'integrist'* position which he reflected. In addition, Pugin, together with his patrons John Hardman (Handsworth Mercy Convent) and the Earl of Shrewsbury (Alton Hospital), was closely involved with the building of what he would have seen as the communities that would provide the solution to these problems. These two projects are among the schemes which he was to publish in *Present State of Ecclesiastical Architecture* (1841-2). The building of his own house and church at Ramsgate, and the artistic, family and religious life conducted there was also intended to be such an ideal, Catholic, patriarchal community, a tradition later to be part imitated by Belloc, Eric Gill and others. His *a priori* religious, moral and ethical criteria for reintegration of architecture and society reflected a totalitarian approach which others were to dedicate to quite different value systems, as David Watkin has shown in *Morality and Architecture* (1977).

Where *Contrasts* was an illustrated manifesto, *True Principles* is more noted for its argument than its plates. It is most famous for its two principles:

'*1st, that there should be no features about a building which are not necessary for convenience, construction, or propriety*;

2nd, that all ornament should consist of enrichment of the essential construction of the building'

and the qualifications 'In pure architecture the smallest detail should *have a meaning or serve a purpose*' [and] 'construction itself *should vary with the material employed*' (p.1).

Applying this 'functionalist' and 'rationalist' critique (inherent in fact in the classical style, and much studied in eighteenth-century France) required that the construction, materials and plan of a building be revealed rather than concealed. It was this 'legibility' or 'reality' which Pugin emphasized and in which he was most closely followed, especially by the Cambridge Camden, later the Ecclesiological, Society, the Anglican church restoration-and-design pressure group whose motto was 'let every material be real ...' (Cambridge Camden Society, *A Few Words to Church Builders* (1841), p. 4). Although that pusillanimous body decided in 1839 not to offer him honorary membership because of 'his notorious Catholicism', his influence on church-architecture, especially in the Anglican context, was to last well into the twentieth century.

The implementation of these principles was, of course, intended to overthrow the neoclassical style and relax the straightjacket of the classical rules of planning and disposing openings on elevation: instead he said: '... the elevation being made subservient to the plan' (p. 63) the opposite of what Barry did at the Houses of Parliament, of which Pugin is supposed to have said 'All Grecian, Sir; Tudor details on a classical body' (B. Ferrey, *Recollections*, p. 248). Pugin was to be at his most influential in reforming the practice of the Gothic Revival and domestic architecture of what, in another context, he called the 'middle class' home, and his revolutionary influence on its construction, planning and decoration was first demonstrated in his own house, St Augustine's Grange, Ramsgate (1843). Pugin thus stands at the wellspring of nineteenth-century architectural and design reform, which was to be reflected in the institution that would become the Victoria & Albert Museum, the publications of Ruskin, and in the architecture and decorative programme of William Morris. In 1888 John Dando Sedding observed, 'we should have had no Morris, no Street, no Burges, no Webb, no Bodley, no Rossetti, no Burne-Jones, no Crane, but for Pugin' (*Art and Handicraft* (1893), p. 144). The paternity of the twentieth-century Modern Movement can be traced back to Pugin and to *True Principles*. But Pugin avoided what Andrew Saint calls its 'vulgar functionalism' by appealing, both in church and domestic architecture, to 'propriety ... *the external and internal appearance of an edifice should be illustrative of, and in accordance with, the purpose for which it is destined*' (*True Principles*, p. 42) and because 'propriety' called for hierarchy and ornament in architecture, this allowed him to indulge his great passion as a decorator (Andrew Saint, 'The Fate of Pugin's *True Principles*', pp. 272–82 in Paul Atterbury and C. Wainwright (eds), *Pugin, a Gothic Passion* (1994), quotation p. 274).

The text of *True Principles of Pointed or Christian Architecture* (Pugin used 'Christian' interchangeably with 'Catholic') was purchased from Pugin and published by the specialist London architectural publisher John Weale on 3 July 1841. He charged Weale £169.17s.0d. There was a remarkably short gestation of the illustrations so vital to his message. Pugin himself cut the copper plates for engraving his nine major plates and thirty-one 'vignettes', which he seems to have produced in collaboration with T.T. Bury between February and March 1841. Pugin was deeply involved in the production of the book, dismissing in February the high cost and inefficiency of woodcutting for his major plates, although insisting on the forty-seven woodcuts being incorporated as figures in the text. (This complicated story is sorted out in M. Belcher, *AWN Pugin, an Annotated Critical Bibliography* (1987) pp. 59–64). By February 1843 Pugin reckoned that over twelve hundred copies had been sold, although he did not get the reviews he had hoped for in the Anglican *British Critic* and the Catholic *Dublin Review*. Nevertheless, in retrospect *True Principles* is the book on which Pugin's reputation as a design reformer must be based, as his first biographer Benjamin Ferrey claimed (*Recollections*, p. 147); Andrew Saint reckons that its hegemony lasted thirty years.

If the plates were produced astonishingly quickly, the text was not. It has been remarked that Pugin's architectural thought did not develop much, and that he restated much the same positions in *Contrasts*, *True Principles* and then in the *Apology* (1843). This is consistent with the understanding that 'Lecture I' and 'Lecture II' into which the book is divided were given some years before. Could these be in fact lectures that he had delivered to the students (both 'church' and lay boys) at St Mary's College, Oscott in 1838–9? Certainly, at least five such lectures were given by him from 1838–9, of which three 'Lectures on ecclesiastical architecture' were published separately in the Catholic periodical press. In the 'Lecture the first' (published in the *Catholic Magazine*, April 1838) Pugin names the monk and bishop builders, such as William of Wykeham, then thought to have been the architects of their churches. These are also found in the chevron bands of the border of the *True Principles* frontispiece, which shows the cloistered, habited, cleric-like architect in his cell. In 'Lecture the second' (June 1838) Pugin's denunciation of the neoclassical style is repeated. Only 'Lecture the third' (January–February 1839) is, like *True Principles*, an architectural or art-historical lecture in the sense we would now understand it. It is concerned with stained glass and its revival and was illustrated with large details drawn on canvas, some of which still survive at Oscott, which anticipate the visual, analytical approach adopted in *True Principles*. 'Lecture I', on the aesthetics – rather than the engineering – of building in stone (pp. 1–20), follows on with this approach, and allows for repetition of his claims of the superiority of the Gothic over the classical style; 'on metalwork' (pp. 20–33) was perhaps another lecture, dealing with structural, base and precious metalwork. Pugin then moves into his favourite area of design reform, with its hits at the tricks of the trade of the

Regency decorator and upholsterer. 'Lecture II' on woodwork (pp. 34–42) deals with timber-framing in walls and roof structures, particularly in decorative aspects. Pugin then departs from the analytical, and turns to what he calls 'decoration with reference to propriety' (p. 42); here his thought becomes more manifesto-like than in the other lectures. Also under the heading 'propriety,' he deals with building types, 'Ecclesiastical, Collegiate, and Civil' (p. 42), the first allowing another denunciation of the classical style as evolved from the Pagan temple, the other two a critique of the neoclassical and the revived Gothic, guying especially the domestic 'Abbey Style' of Fonthill, which he contrasts with the 'Catholic England was merry England' style of medieval manor house building (pp. 59–61) and thus once again he moves off into social and religious criticism. He also introduces a nationalist justification for the Gothic – 'we are not Italians, we are Englishmen' (p. 56) – comments on the plan in relation to elevations (pp. 59–62), and finally on the effects of scale (pp. 63–7).

There is little specifically Catholic polemic about this book: there was, after all, plenty of that in the second edition of *Contrasts* which was published almost simultaneously. The woodcut of the modern college (p. 54) is something of a dig at the two Catholic seminary buildings from the 1790s – St Edmund's, Ware, and Ushaw – and is contrasted with the birds-eye view of Magdalen College, Oxford, where Pugin was shortly to build a new gateway (1844). Perhaps he hoped that a less confessional, less polemical work might broaden his contacts and open up lines of communication with the 'Oxford Men'. It certainly had its Catholic plagiarism in the form of a pirated French language edition, *Les Vrais Principes* (Paris/Bruges 1850), which included some of Pugin's own schemes never published in England, and stands at the beginning of Pugin's enormous influence in Belgium (rather than France).

An Apology for the Revival of Christian Architecture, was published two years later in 1843. Once again the publisher was Weale, and letters to him with some preparatory drawings are in the British Library. It shows *True Principles* to be (for Pugin) the sort of consistent and disciplined argument called for by the lecture form; *An Apology* is much more random. Had the themes been better arranged, it might have had similar authority. These are (not in order of their appearance) Pugin's revised and much more sympathetic view of the Church of England (pp. 25–31, 35, 47–51) which shows an almost millenarian expectation of a 'Re-Union' (not Pugin's phrase) of the Anglican Communion with the Catholic Church. This is contrasted with a sharper denunciation of the suicide of the English Medieval Catholic Church during the Reformation Parliament (1529–32) – 'the people were actually betrayed by their own lawful pastors' (p. 46) – and the Dissolution of the Monasteries (1536–9), which argument also appeared in *Contrasts* (1841). Allied to this is Pugin's romantic, 'Merry England' view of the English constitution (pp. 37, 45–7), entirely glossing over the realities of early nineteenth-century Britain, so acerbically analyzed in the two pairs of plates which he added to the 1841 edition of *Contrasts*, which are some of the strongest Pugin ever drew. In 'The Catholic town in 1440' contrasted with 'the same town in 1840' the sixteen places of worship of 1440 are reduced to a mere handful, but now in competition with 'Mr. Evans' chapel, Baptist chapel, Unitarian chapel, Wesleyan chapel, New Christian Society, Quakers meeting, Socialist Hall of Science', demonstrating, the break up of architectural and religious unity consequent on the Reformation. The 'Contrasted residences of the poor: modern poor house [and] ancient poorhouse', attacks the workhouse system, that newly perfected example of early nineteenth-century Utilitarian social engineering, against the supposed lavish provision in the Middle Ages. Following the mood of *Contrasts*, Pugin attacks individual buildings at Oxford and Cambridge (pp. 3, 33), the Euston and Curzon Street, Birmingham, terminuses of the London & Birmingham Railway, on which he travelled incessantly (pp. 10–12), the new Gothic buildings of Christ's Hospital, London, and Blore's new buildings at Lambeth Palace (pp. 14–15), the Bank of England (pp. 16–17), and Tite's Royal Exchange (pp. 18–19). Pugin blames all their faults on an architectural education (p. 19), which he had guyed in *Contrasts* in the plate, 'dedicated without permission to THE TRADE', showing an architect's office, or rather shop, plastered with posters such as 'Wanted. A youth to prick off designs in an eminent office'.

Architectural education was still based on pupilship and the study of the classical Orders and, for the most privileged, the investigative archaeological tour of ancient sites, such as the 1842 Cambridge University 'travelling bachelor' award to F. C. Penrose, the Magdalene College, Cambridge undergraduate, who in 1835 applied to Pugin for advice on an architectural career (but was instead recommended to apply to Blore). Pugin instead proposed an English so-called 'archaeological' education, based on studying the English provinces and their buildings (this was in fact achieved by the Committee set up in 1862 to commemorate Pugin which established the RIBA Pugin Travelling Studentship, abolished *c.*1970). Pugin himself did not take on pupils, and the quip 'Clerk, my dear Sir, clerk, I never employ one; I would kill him within a week' (B. Ferrey, p. 187) and the aside in the *Apology* about stopping up and fusing architectural offices 'as they serve wasps' nests in the country' (p. 20), show his continued detachment from 'the Trade'. He denounced architecture as taught at the Royal Academy Schools (the only regular public architectural education then available), and it is in this context that his comment on the work of C. R. Cockerell (Professor of

Architecture at the RA 1839–56) at Oxford and Cambridge should be seen: 'a man who paganizes *in the Universities* deserves no quarter' (p. 3). With his plea for the study of English models, Pugin is going further than asking for the sort of architectural recording accuracy achieved in *Examples*, saying 'I trust, before long, to produce a treatise on *Natural Architecture*' (p. 15) based on regional studies (p. 20) and local materials and building types (p. 21), such as 'the peasant's hut, the yeoman's cottage ...' and even the proto-Ruskinian recommendation: 'be a minute observer of the animal and vegetable creation, of the grand effects of nature ... stores ... rich for the natural architect' (p. 21). Although no book on 'natural bulding' resulted, the study of the local and vernacular was to characterize the best domestic work of the Gothic Revival and later nineteenth- and early twentieth-century architects such as Shaw, Lutyens and Voysey.

Interestingly, Pugin thought that railway building and engineering should have produced 'Natural architecture' – 'the Railways, had they been naturally treated, [would have] afforded a fine scope for grand massive architecture' (p. 10) – but the actual results are caricatured in Plate III. Some structure can be traced in *An Apology's* remarks on other building types, cemetery architecture (p. 12) 'ecclesiastical architecture', including that of colleges (pp. 31–3), hospitals and almshouses (p. 33), 'Civil architecture' (referring to 'smaller detached houses which the present state of society has generated' (p. 38) that is the middle-class professional house) but the argument tends to run away rather than be analytical or prescriptive. Finally, under the heading 'Sculpture', where he gives his views on funerary monuments, Pugin shows that he knows the work of Giotto (Plate IX) and of the German Nazarene painter Overbeck (p. 44), who is also noticed in the 1841 edition of *Contrasts*, and that his interest in the Italian Primitives anticipates that of the Pre-Raphaelite Brotherhood, founded in 1848.

Writing to an Anglican correspondent, Pugin called the *Apology* 'a sort of tract for the times', the title of the series of pamphlets at that time rocking the Anglican Church. This comment, the dedication to Lord Shrewsbury, and the attack on architectural education give us a clue as to what Pugin intended the *Apology* to be: a tract on the state of the architectural profession and the Catholic Church. The model he held up instead was the 'English Catholic' Church project of himself and Lord Shrewsbury, of which the fruits are given as the Frontispiece and Plate III, rather than as explained in the text. The frontispiece 'the Present Revival of Christian Architecture' shows twenty-five of the thirty-five church projects with which Pugin had been involved since 1835, one of them fully and many partly funded by Shrewsbury. Pugin's plate is also a repost to C. R. Cockerell's magisterial watercolour composition *A Tribute to the Memory of*

Sir Christopher Wren, exhibited at the RA in 1838, which similarly shows Wren's churches in serried ranks and deepening perspective. Pugin cleverly positions the unbuilt tower and spire of his St George's, Southwark, centrally in the plate, allowing it to dominate and thus foreshorten the long, low, spreading effect of the actual three-aisle church then under construction – he was not above employing the tricks of the perspectivist's art when it came to presenting his own work. (The tower and spire was never completed, although Pugin exhibited a watercolour of it at the RA in 1849). And such churches and their liturgies were to be furnished with the stained glass and base and precious metal work as shown in Plate X 'Church Furniture revived at Birmingham'. (As usual the text has much on metal work, both structural and decorative, particularly on the ledger brasses revived by Hardman & Co.). The text, however, almost refutes the progress these plates establish: he is wonderfully dismissive of the actual state of the Catholic Church in England and Ireland (p. 23) on which he was particularly outspoken: its architecture is still guyed as Italian (pp. 22–5) its music (p. 24) and its journalism (p. 24) dismissed, allowing nothing for the progress that his own churches, their liturgical openings or his journalism represented. Catholic factiousness (p. 47), and the political alliance with Nonconformity and with radicalism at the hustings (p. 51) (a veiled reference to the Irish nationalist leader Daniel O'Connell, who particularly annoyed Lord Shrewsbury) are also denounced.

An Apology does not add significantly to Pugin's reputation, and it can be very frustrating to use. New ideas on 'natural architecture', on the influence of climate (pp. 21–2), and even the claim that the development of the Gothic (pp. 6–7) was inherent in earlier styles such as the 'Lombard' ('Development', that is to say, in Newman's sense) are introduced tantalizingly rather than developed. And it tells us nothing about Pugin's actual buildings nor does it quantify the patronage of the Earl of Shrewsbury which made them possible, except by implication that he is the most generous Catholic patron, in contrast to his peers (literally), the clergy and the apathetic people. For this information one has to go to Pugin's *Present State* issued in book form in 1843. But *inter alia* Pugin defines the two guiding, integral principles of his own life: that he who makes 'the study of Catholic antiquity ... is ... drawn from the contemplation of material objects to spiritual truths' (p. 49), and that 'it is not a *style*, but a *principle*' for which he fought (p. 44).

True Principles (1841) was reprinted in 1853, in 1895 and in the mid twentieth century; the original manuscript is in the Metropolitan Museum, New York. *An Apology* (1843) was reprinted in 1895 and in 1969; the 1843 edition is usually found bound with *True Principles* (in the 1853 reprint) so it seems historically appropriate to re-issue them once again as one volume, but here using the 1841 edition of *True Principles*. This, the first twenty-first century joint edition is intended to make more widely available to the historian and student, as well as for Victorian Studies, two of Pugin's key texts, written within two years of each other at a crucial time in the development of his architectural vision as articulated in print.

Roderick O'Donnell
Feast of Holy Cross 2003

The true principles of pointed architecture

London. Published by John Weale. 59. High Holborn. 1841.

THE TRUE PRINCIPLES

OF

Pointed or Christian Architecture:

SET FORTH IN

TWO LECTURES DELIVERED AT ST. MARIE'S, OSCOTT,

BY

A. WELBY PUGIN,

ARCHITECT,

AND PROFESSOR OF ECCLESIASTICAL ANTIQUITIES IN THAT COLLEGE.

LONDON: JOHN WEALE.

M.CCM.XLI.

𝕷𝖔𝖓𝖉𝖔𝖓:

PRINTED BY W. HUGHES, KING'S HEAD COURT, GOUGH SQUARE.

THE INK SUPPLIED BY MESSRS. SHACKELL AND LYONS.

LIST OF PLATES.

47 WOOD-CUTS.

31 VIGNETTES.

——

78

PRINCIPLES

OF

POINTED OR CHRISTIAN ARCHITECTURE.

LECTURE I.

The object of the present Lecture is to set forth and explain the true principles of Pointed or Christian Architecture, by the knowledge of which you may be enabled to test architectural excellence. The two great rules for design are these: *1st, that there should be no features about a building which are not necessary for convenience, construction, or propriety; 2nd, that all ornament should consist of enrichment of the essential construction of the building.* The neglect of these two rules is the cause of all the bad architecture of the present time. Architectural features are continually tacked on buildings with which they have no connexion, merely for the sake of what is termed effect; and ornaments are *actually constructed*, instead of forming the decoration of *construction*, to which in good taste they should be always subservient.

In pure architecture the smallest detail should *have a meaning or serve a purpose;* and even the construction itself *should vary with the material employed*, and the designs should be adapted to the material in which they are executed.

Strange as it may appear at first sight, it is in *pointed architecture alone that these great principles have been carried out;* and I shall be able to illustrate them from the vast cathedral to the simplest erection. Moreover, the architects of the middle ages were the first who *turned the natural properties of the various materials to their full account,* and made *their mechanism a vehicle for their art.*

We shall have therefore to consider ornament with reference to construction and convenience, and ornament with reference to architectural propriety. Construction must be subdivided and treated under three distinct heads,—stone, timber, and metal; brick might indeed be added, but as the principles of its construction are similar to those of stone, I shall not make any distinction; and as for plaster, when used for any other purpose than coating walls, it is a mere modern deception, and the trade is not worthy of a distinction.

To begin with stone. A pointed church is the masterpiece of masonry. It is essentially a stone building; its pillars, its arches, its vaults, its intricate intersections, its ramified tracery, are all peculiar to stone, and could not be consistently executed in any other material. Moreover, the ancient masons obtained great altitude and great extent with a surprising economy of wall and substance; the wonderful strength and solidity of their buildings are the result, not of the *quantity or size of the stones* employed, but of the *art of their disposition.* To exhibit the great excellence of these constructions, it will be here necessary to draw a comparison between them and those of the far-famed classic shores of Greece. Grecian architecture is essentially *wooden* in its construction; it originated in wooden buildings, and never did its professors possess either sufficient imagination or skill to conceive any departure from the original type. Vitruvius shows that their buildings were formerly composed of trunks of trees, with lintels or brestsummers laid across the top, and rafters again resting on them. This is at once the most ancient and barbarous mode of building that can be imagined; it is heavy, and, as I before said, essentially wooden; but is it not extraordinary that when the Greeks commenced building in stone, the *properties of this material did*

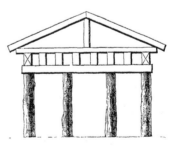

A Wooden Building the origin of Greek Temples.

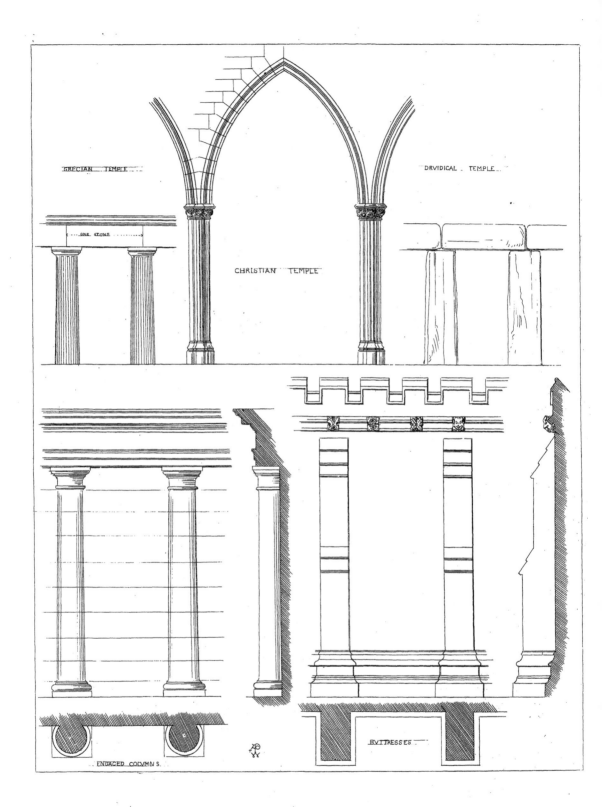

GRECIAN TEMPLE

ONE STONE

CHRISTIAN TEMPLE

DRVIDICAL TEMPLE

ENGAGED COLVMNS

BVTTRESSES

Plate 1.

London Published by John Weale. 59. High Holborn. 1841.

not suggest to them some different and improved mode of construction?
Such, however, was not the case; they set up stone pillars as they had
set up trunks of wood; they laid stone lintels as they had laid wood
ones, *flat across;* they even made the construction appear still more
similar to wood, by carving triglyphs, which are merely a representation of
the beam ends. The finest temple of the Greeks is constructed on the
same principle as a large wooden cabin. As illustrations of history they
are extremely valuable; but as for their being held up as the standard
of architectural excellence, and the types from which our present buildings
are to be formed, it is a monstrous absurdity, which has originated in the
blind admiration of modern times for every thing Pagan, to the prejudice
and overthrow of Christian art and propriety.

The Greeks erected their columns, like the uprights of Stonehenge, just
so far apart that the blocks *they laid on them would not break by their own
weight.* The Christian architects, on the contrary, during the *dark ages,*
with stone scarcely larger than ordinary bricks, threw their lofty vaults
from slender pillars across a vast intermediate space, and that at an
amazing height, where they had every difficulty of lateral pressure to contend with. This leads me to speak of buttresses, a distinguishing feature
of Pointed Architecture, and the first we shall consider in detail.—Plate I.

It need hardly be remarked that buttresses are necessary supports to a
lofty wall. A wall of three feet in thickness, with buttresses projecting
three feet more at intervals, is much stronger than a wall of six feet thick
without buttresses. A long unbroken mass of building without light
and shade is monotonous and unsightly; it is evident, therefore, that
both for strength and beauty, breaks or projections are necessary in
architecture. We will now examine in which style, Christian or Pagan,
these have been most successfully carried out. Pointed architecture
does *not conceal her construction, but beautifies it:* classic architecture
seeks to conceal instead of decorating it, and therefore has resorted to
the use of engaged columns as breaks for strength and effect;—nothing
can be worse. A column is an architectural member which should only

be employed when a superincumbent weight is required to be sustained *without the obstruction of a solid wall;* but the moment a wall is built, the *necessity and propriety of columns cease,* and engaged columns always produce the effect of having once been detached, and the intermediate spaces blocked up afterwards.

A buttress in pointed architecture at once shows its purpose, and diminishes naturally as it rises and has less to resist. An engaged column, on the contrary, is overhung by a cornice. A buttress, by means of water tables, can be made to project such a distance as to produce a fine effect of light and shade. An engaged column can never project far on account of the cornice, and all the other members, necessarily according with the diameter of the column, would be increased beyond all proportion. I will now leave you to judge in which style the real intention of a buttress is best carried out.

Flying Buttresses.

I have yet to speak of flying buttresses, those bold arches, as their name implies, by which the lateral thrust of the nave groining is thrown over the aisles and transferred to the massive lower buttresses. Here again we see the true principles of Christian architecture, by the conversion of an essential support of the building into a light and elegant decoration. Who can stand among the airy arches of Amiens, Cologne, Chartres, Beauvais, or Westminster, and not be filled with admiration at the mechanical skill and beautiful combination of form which are united in their construction? But, say the modern critics, they are only props, and a bungling contrivance. Let us examine this. Are the revived pagan buildings constructed with such superior skill as to dispense with these supports? By no means; the clumsy vaults of St. Paul's, London, mere coffered semi-arches, without ribs or intersections, *have their flying buttresses; but as this style of architecture does not admit of the great principle of decorating utility*, these buttresses, instead of being made *ornamental, are concealed by an enormous screen*, going entirely round *the building. So that in fact one half of the edifice is built to conceal the other.* Miserable expedient! worthy only of the debased style in which it has been resorted to.

Section of a Pointed Church, with the Flying Buttresses decorated.

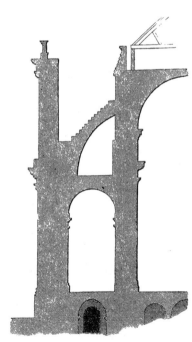

Section of St. Paul's, London, a Church built in the revived Pagan style, with the Flying Buttresses concealed by a Screen.

It is proper to remark that the cluster of pinnacles at A are not carried up for *mere ornament*, but, by their *weight*, to increase the resistance of the great pinnacle at the point of thrust.

We will now proceed, in the second place, to consider groining and vaulting, which are solely adapted to stone construction.

A groined ceiling is divided into compartments by means of ribs springing from caps or corbels, and uniting in bosses placed at the intersections ; the spaces between the ribs are termed spandrils : the word boss signifies a spring of water, and has doubtless been applied to the key-stones of vaults, as the ribs seem to spring or separate from them.

Here again the great principle of decorating utility is to be observed. A stone ceiling is most essential in a large church, both for durability, security from fire,[1] and conveyance of sound. It is impossible to conceive stone ceilings better contrived than those of the ancient churches ; they are at once light, substantial, beautiful, and lofty. 1st. They are light, because, their principal strength lying in the ribs, the intermediate spaces or spandrils are filled in with small light stones. 2nd. They are substantial, for all the stones being cut to a centre and forming portions of

a curve, when united they are capable of resisting immense pressure, the keys or bosses wedging all together. 3rd. They are beautiful, for no ceiling can be conceived more graceful and elegant than a long perspective of lines and arches radiating from exquisitely carved centres. 4th. They are lofty, not only on account of the elevation at which they are placed, but that their construction permits the clerestory windows to be carried up level with the crown of the arch in the intermediate spaces.

[1] Within the last few years the roofs have been burnt off the cathedrals of Rouen, Chartres, and Bruges ; and, owing to the strength of the stone vaulting, the interiors of these churches have scarcely been injured ; while York Minster has twice been completely

In the groining of the later styles we find a great departure from the severe and consistent principles I have been describing. Henry the Seventh's Chapel at Westminster is justly considered one of the most wonderful examples of ingenious construction and elaborate fan groining in the world, but at the same time it exhibits the commencement of the bad taste, by *constructing its ornament instead of confining it to the enrichment of its construction.* I allude to the stone pendants of the ceiling, which are certainly extravagances. A key-stone is *necessary* for

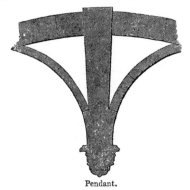

Pendant.

Boss.

the support of arched ribs; the older architects contented themselves with enriching it with foliage or figures, but those of the later styles allowed four or five feet of *unnecessary stone to hang down into the church*, and from it to branch other ribs upwards. This is at most an ingenious trick, and quite unworthy of the severity of Pointed or Christian architecture.[2]

---

gutted within a short period through the want of a stone groining; and yet a mere wood and plaster ceiling has been again constructed!

[2] This is one among many other symptoms of decline apparent in the later works in the pointed style. The moment the *flat* or *four-centred arch* was introduced, the spirit of Christian architecture was on the wane. *Height* or the *vertical principle*, emblematic of the resurrection, is the very essence of Christian architecture. It was to attain greater elevation with a given width that the pointed arch was employed; and the four-centred arch does not possess equal advantage in this respect with the old semi; and although some of the later buildings, as King's College Chapel, Cambridge, still retain the principle of internal height, with the use of the depressed arch, yet who can avoid being struck with the inconsistency of

In the third place, we will proceed to the use and intention of pinnacles and spiral terminations. I have little doubt that pinnacles are considered

running up walls to a prodigious elevation, and then, instead of *carrying out the principle, and springing a lofty groin*, losing a considerable increase of height by a flattened thrusting arched ceiling; the form of which is a sort of contradiction to the height at which it is commenced.

I do not make this observation by way of disparaging the merits of this stupendous building, but merely to show the early decay of the true principles of pointed architecture which may be traced even in that glorious pile.

We not unfrequently find the bulbous form employed in the Tudor period: this, which afterwards became the prevailing form of the Dresden and Flemish steeples, is of *the worst possible taste; and why?* Because *it is a form which does not result from any consistent mode of constructing a covering*, and, on the contrary, requires by its shape *to be constructed*, as will be seen by the annexed sketch; by the side of which I have placed a spire, the severe form and decoration of which are quite consistent with the true principles of rendering the necessary roof or covering of a tower elegant in appearance, without *departing* from *essential construction* for the sake of *ornament*.

One of the greatest defects of St. Paul's, London, is its fictitious dome. *The dome that is seen* is not *the dome of the church*, but a mere construction for effect. At St. Peter's the dome *is the actual covering of the building*, and is therefore constructed in that respect on the true principle; but, as will be perceived by the an-

Bulbous Covering or Steeple, in the debased style.

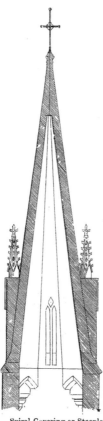

Spiral Covering or Steeple, in the Christian style.

by the majority of persons as mere ornamental excrescences, introduced solely for picturesque effect. The very reverse of these is the case ; and I shall be able to show you that their introduction is warranted by the soundest principles of construction and design. They should be regarded 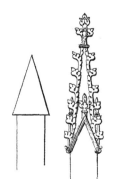 as answering a double intention, both mystical and natural : their mystical intention is, like other vertical lines and terminations of Christian architecture, to represent an emblem of the Resurrection ; their natural intention is that of an upper weathering, to throw off rain. The most useful covering for this purpose, and the one that would naturally suggest itself, is of the form represented in the annexed figure : only let this *essential form* be *decorated* with a finial and crockets, and we have at once a perfect pinnacle. Now the square piers of which these floriated tops form the terminations are all erected to answer a useful purpose ; when they rise

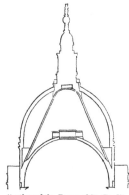

Section of the Dome of St. Paul's.

nexed section, the upper part of St. Paul's is mere imposing show, constructed at a vast expense without any legitimate reason.

From the various symptoms of decline which I have shown to have existed in the later pointed works, I feel convinced that Christian architecture had gone its length, and it must necessarily have destroyed itself by departing from its own principles in the pursuit of novelty, or it must have fallen back on its pure and ancient models. This is quite borne out by existing facts. Now that the pointed style is reviving, we cannot successfully suggest any thing new, but are obliged to return to the spirit of the ancient work. Indeed, if we view pointed architecture in its true light as Christian art, as the faith itself *is perfect, so are the principles on which it is founded.* We may indeed improve in mechanical contrivances to expedite its execution, we may even increase its scale and grandeur ; but we can *never successfully deviate one tittle from the spirit and principles* of pointed architecture. We must rest content to *follow*, not to *lead ;* we may indeed widen the road which our Catholic forefathers formed, but we can never depart from their track without a certainty of failure being the result of our presumption.

from the tops of wall buttresses, they serve as piers to strengthen the parapet, which would be exceedingly weak without some such support. Fig. S.

Their utility on the great piers which resist the flying buttresses has been already mentioned under the head of buttress. At the bases of great spires, the clusters of pinnacles are also placed to increase strength and resistance; in short, wherever pinnacles are introduced in pure pointed architecture, they will be found on examination to fulfil a useful end.

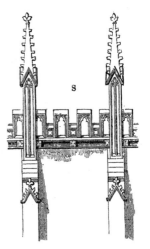

The same remarks will apply to the crocketed and floriated terminations of staircase and other turrets, which are in fact ornamented roofs; and I need hardly remark that turrets were not carried up without a legitimate reason.

Every tower built during the pure style of pointed architecture either was, or was intended to be, surmounted by a spire, which is the natural covering for a tower; a flat roof is both contrary to the spirit of the style, and it is also practically bad. There is no instance before the year 1400 of a church tower being erected without *the intention at least* of being covered or surmounted by a spire; and those towers antecedent to that period which we find without such terminations have either been left incomplete for want of funds, weakness in the sub-structure, or some casual impediment,—or the spires, which were often of timber covered with lead, have been pulled down for the sake of their material.[3] In fine, when towers were erected with flat embattled tops, *Christian architecture*

---

[3] The following glorious churches have been stripped of their spires since the views in Dugdale's Monasticon were taken:—Hereford Cathedral, Worcester Cathedral, Southwell Minster, Rochester Cathedral, Ely Cathedral, Ripon Minster, Finchal Abbey, and Lincoln Cathedral. It is to be remembered that these views were taken *above a century after the lead-stripping and spire-demolishing period commenced.*

was on the decline, and the omission of the ancient and appropriate termination was strong evidence of that fact. Towers surmounting gatehouses were never terminated by spires, for, being originally built for defence, the space at top was required for that purpose. This is the real reason why square-topped and embattled towers are said to be of a domestic character; so that even by persons unacquainted with the use and intentions of spires, they are associated with the idea of ecclesiastical architecture.

The pitch of roof in pointed architecture is another subject on which some useful observations may be made. It will be found, on examination, that the most beautiful pitch of a roof or gable end is an inclination sufficiently steep to throw off snow without giving the slate or lead covering *too perpendicular a strain*, which is formed by two sides on an equilateral triangle.

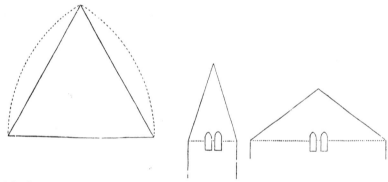

If this form be departed from, the gable appears either painfully acute or too widely spread. All really beautiful forms in architecture are based on the soundest principles of utility.

Practical men know that flat-pitched roofs, which are exceedingly ugly in appearance, are also but ill calculated to resist the action of weather. In slated roofs especially, gusts of wind actually blow under and lift up the covering: when the pitch is increased to its proper elevation, the whole pressure of the wind is *lateral*, and forces the covering closer to the roof.

I now come to speak, in the fourth place, of mouldings, on the judicious form and disposition of which a very considerable part of the effect of the building depends.   Mouldings are the enrichment of splays of doorways,

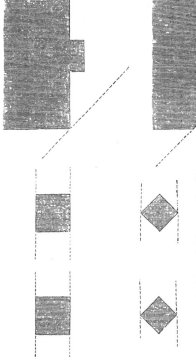

windows, arches, and piers, of base and string-courses, of weatherings and copings, and they are introduced solely on the principle of decorating the useful.

I will first point out the necessity of these splays and weatherings, and then proceed to consider the form and application of mouldings to them.

It will be readily seen that without a splay a considerable portion of light would be excluded, and that this form of jamb is necessary to the use and intention of a window.

In a doorway the convenience of splayed sides must be evident for ordinary ingress and egress. This form of jamb is therefore necessary to the use and intention of a doorway.

The advantage of piers splayed, or placed diagonally over square ones, both for elegance and convenience, must be evident to all; the arch mould over them

Square Piers supporting
Arches.

Splayed Piers supporting
Arches.

is consequently splayed. This form of pier and arch mould is therefore necessary for both piers and arches.

Great increase of solidity and strength is gained by projections at the

base of a building as sets-off; but were these projections left flat at top instead of being bevelled off, they would become lodgments for water.

The splayed or bevelled form is therefore necessary for base moulds. Strings and copings, the very intention of which is to throw off water, must be sloped, for the same reason.

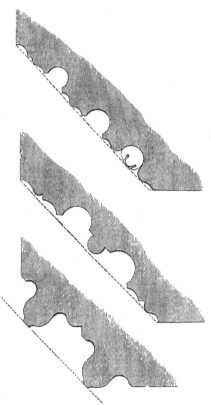

Examples of ancient Jamb Moulds.

The use of the splayed form being now demonstrated, I will proceed to consider the mouldings used to enrich it. All mouldings should be designed on the principle of light, shadow, and half tint; and the section of a moulding should be of such a form as to produce various and pleasing gradations of light and shadow. Monotony should be carefully avoided, also all cutting shadows near the outer edge, which have a meagre effect. The original splayed form should never be lost sight of in the sinkings of the mould, which ought not to be so extravagantly deep as to produce both a real and apparent weakness in the jamb.

All the mouldings of jamb are *invariably sunk from the face of the work.* A projecting mould in such a situation would be a useless excrescence, and contrary to the principles of pointed architecture, which do not admit of any unnecessary members. A hood mould projects immediately above the springing of the arch to receive the water running down the wall over the window, and convey it off on either side. This projection

Examples of ancient Jamb Moulds.

answers a purpose, and therefore is not only allowable but indispensable in the pointed style; but a projection down the sides of jamb, where it would be utterly useless, is never found among the monuments of antiquity.

Modern Jamb Mould, weak and wiry.

French Jamb Mould of the late styles, *extravagantly* hollowed.

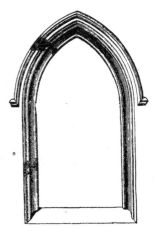

The mouldings round an arch are generally more subdivided than those of the jamb. This is carrying out the same principle that may be observed in vegetation, where the solid trunk spreads and divides as it rises upwards. The use of caps at the springing of arches is to receive the different moulds of jamb and arch, which could not be successfully united by any better means than foliated and moulded projections. Hence, in the later pointed continental churches, where the same moulds run up the jambs and round the arches without interruption, caps are entirely omitted; and the same thing is observable, under similar

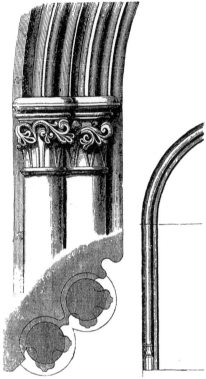

Caps at the transition from Jamb to Arch Mould.

circumstances, in the nave of Crowland Abbey, Lincolnshire.

The next class of mouldings I will notice are those belonging to base moulds, weatherings, and strings. I have shown above that the bevelled form is necessary for these projections; but when the weathering is of any depth, it is evident that the inclined plane cut by the horizontal joints of the masonry will produce what are technically called feather-edged joints, at A A A, which would be easily broken by the action of frost, and the joints themselves would be penetrated by water. To obviate this, all the varied and beautiful

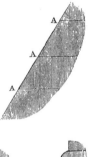

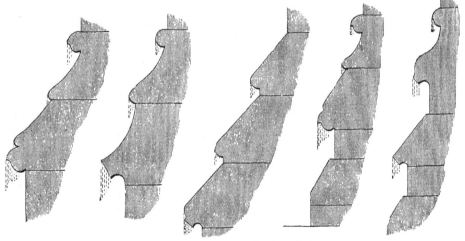

Ancient examples of Base Moulds and Weatherings.

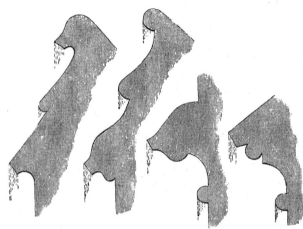

moulds of weatherings have been introduced, by the form of which the stones are strengthened at the joints, and they are protected from the action of water by the over-hanging mould throwing it off to the next bevel.

These observations will apply equally to string-courses and copings.

Another important consideration relative to mouldings, and by which their profile should in a great measure be regulated, is the position in which they are placed with relation to the eye of the spectator. The

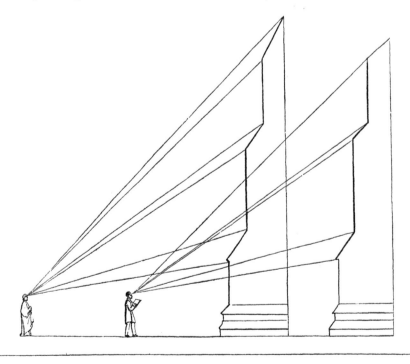

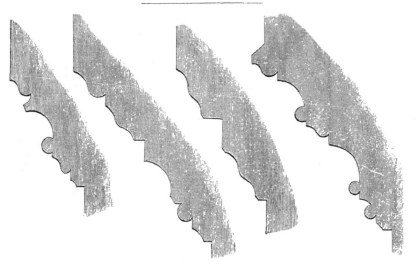

Ancient Profiles of Corbel Moulds.

slope of weatherings themselves is determined by this principle, the pitch increasing with the height that they are placed from the ground. Were this not attended to, the upper water table would be lost to a spectator, unless he was at a considerable distance from the building.

In corbel moulds the profile should *be so formed as to gain projection with strength,*

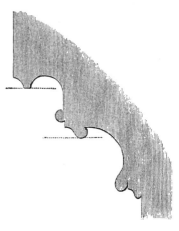

Modern and Weak Corbel Mould.

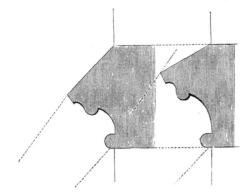

avoiding deep hollows and unnecessary nozings.

The apparent width of a stringcourse placed above the eye depends almost as much on the top bevel as on its actual width; for string-courses of equal width, with different bevels, will vary considerably to the eye.

Every moulding in a pointed building must be designed and shaped on these consistent principles. The severity of Christian architecture requires a *reasonable purpose for the introduction of the smallest detail*, and daily experience proves that those who attempt this glorious style without any fixed idea of its unalterable rules, are certain to end in miserable failures.

Another most important, but now most neglected part of masonry, is the jointing of the stones. All bond and solidity is frequently sacrificed for what is called a neat joint, by setting one stone on end to form a jamb (Plate II. fig. A), when the same space in good old constructions would have been occupied by five or six stones tailing into the wall, and *lying in their natural bed* (fig. B); a point which should be most strictly attended to.

Or, if the jambs are built in courses, they are made as uniform as possible, like rustics (fig. C). By this means the effect of the window is spoiled; the eye, owing to the regularity of these projections, *is carried from the line of jamb to them*, while in the old masonry (fig. D) the irregular outline of the stones does not interfere with the mouldings of the window.

Another point to be remarked in the ancient masonry is the smallness of the stones employed: now, independently of this being the strongest mode of construction, it adds considerably to the effect of the building by increasing its apparent scale. *Large stones destroy proportion;* and to illustrate this I have given two representations of the same piece of architecture differently jointed. Figs. E, F.

Not only are the stones which are used in the ancient buildings exceedingly small, but they are also very irregular in size, and for the same reason as I have before mentioned, that the jointing might *not appear a regular feature*, and by its *lines interfere* with those of the building.

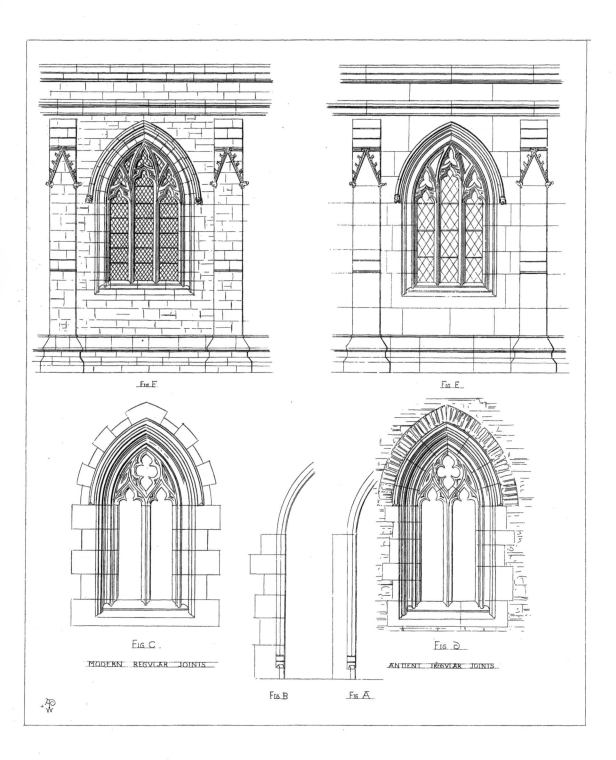

FIG F.

FIG E.

FIG C.

MODERN REGULAR JOINTS

FIG B

FIG A

FIG D.

ANTIENT IRREGULAR JOINTS

Plate II.

London, Published by John Weale, 59, High Holborn, 1841.

In the early buildings the work was carried up in regular beds: there were as many joints in a detached pillar as in the wall, and equal space was occupied by the mortar in every part of the building. The joints of stone tracery should always be cut to the centre of the curve where they fall; and if the joint crosses three or four different *curves, its bed should vary with those curves;* and without this is rigidly adhered to in the construction

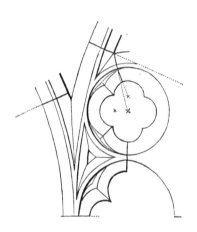

of stone tracery, the work must be devoid of the necessary strength. Any of the great circular or mullioned windows of the ancient cathedrals will fully illustrate this principle.

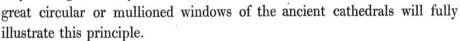

Images in these northern countries were, with some very few exceptions, placed in niches under canopies. This is really necessary to preserve the sculpture from the injuries of weather, and it is much more consistent than leaving the venerable image of a saintly or royal personage exposed to all the pelting of the pitiless storm. Detached images, surmounting buildings, are characteristic of southern and Italian architecture, and are much better suited to the climate of Milan than that of England.

Having now, I trust, successfully shown that the ornamental parts of pointed stone buildings are merely the decorations of their essential construction, and that the formations of mouldings and details are regulated by practical utility, I will endeavour to illustrate the same principles in ancient metal and wood-work.

ON METAL-WORK.

We now come to the consideration of works in metal; and I shall be able to show that the same principles of suiting the design to the material and decorating construction were strictly adhered to by the artists of the middle ages in all their productions in metal, whether precious or common.

In the first place, hinges, locks, bolts, nails, &c., which are always *concealed in modern designs*, were rendered in pointed architecture *rich and beautiful decorations;* and this not only in the doors and fittings of buildings, but in cabinets and small articles of furniture.

The early hinges covered the whole face of the doors with varied and flowing scroll-work. Of this description are those of Notre Dame at Paris, St. Elizabeth's church at Marburg, the western doors of Litchfield Cathedral, the Chapter House at York, and hundreds of other churches, both in England and on the continent. Plate III. figs. 1 and 3.

Hinges of this kind are not only beautiful in design, but they are *practically good*. We all know that on the principle of a lever a door may be easily torn off its modern hinges by a strain applied at its outward edge, (fig. 2.) This could not be the case with the ancient hinges, which extended the whole width of the door, and were bolted through in various

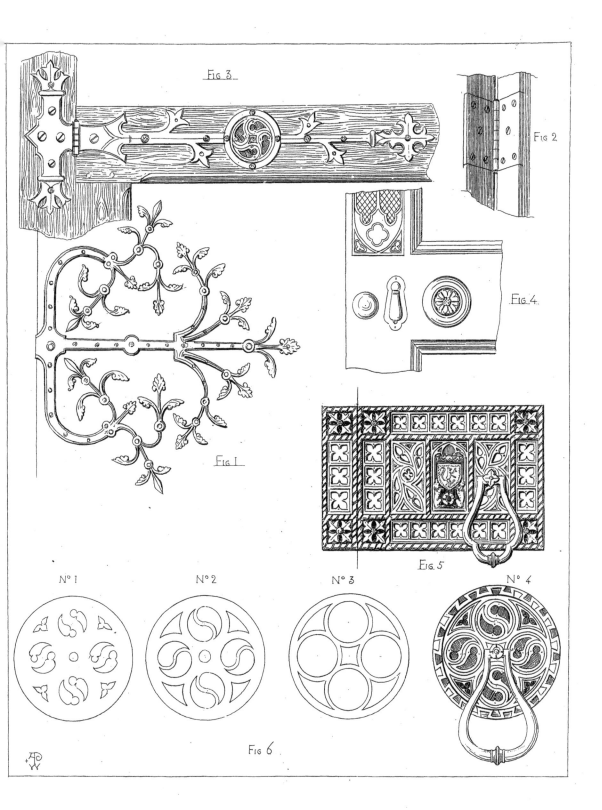

FIG 3.

FIG 2

FIG 4.

FIG 1

FIG 5

Nº 1

Nº 2

Nº 3

Nº 4

FIG 6

Plate III.

London, Published by John Weale, 59. High Holborn, 1841.

FIG 1

FIG 2

FIG 3

FIG 6

FIG 7

MODERN CAST RAILING

FIG 4

ANTIENT RAILING

FIG 5

Plate IV.

London, Published by John Weale, 59, High Holborn, 18.p.

places. In barn-doors and gates these hinges are still used, although devoid of any elegance of form; but they have been most religiously banished from public edifices as unsightly, merely on account of our present race of artists not exercising the same ingenuity as those of ancient times in rendering the *useful* a vehicle for the beautiful: the same remarks will apply to locks that are now concealed and let into the styles of doors, which are often more than half cut away to receive them. Plate III. fig. 4.

A lock was a subject on which the ancient smiths delighted to exercise the utmost resources of their art. The locks of chests were generally of a most elaborate and beautiful description. A splendid example of an old lock still remains at Beddington Manor House, Surrey, and is engraved in my father's work of Examples. In churches we not unfrequently find locks adorned with sacred subjects chased on them, with the most ingenious mechanical contrivances for concealing the key-hole. Keys were also highly ornamented with appropriate decorations referring to the locks to which they belonged; and even the wards turned into beautiful devices and initial letters. Fig. 5.

In all the ancient ornamental iron-work we may discern a peculiar manner of execution, admirably suited to the material, and quite distinct from that of stone or wood. For instance, tracery was produced by different thicknesses of pierced plates laid over each other. Fig. 6.

Leaves and crockets were not *carved* or *modelled*, and *then cast*, but cut out of thin metal plate, and twisted up with pliers (Plate IV. figs. 1, 2), and the lines of stems either engraved or soldered on. By these simple means all the lightness, ease, and sharpness of real vegetation is produced at a much less cost than the heavy flat foliage usually cast and chased up. It is likewise to be remarked, that the necessary fastenings for iron-work were always shown and ornamented. Bolts, nails, and rivets, so far from being unsightly, are beautiful studs and busy enrichments, if properly treated. Fig. 3.

Large tracery was either formed of round iron, like a stem twisted into intersections, or of flat iron bars of different thicknesses riveted together, and the edges chamfered by filing.

Well at Antwerp.

Railings were not *casts of meagre stone tracery* (Plate IV. fig. 4), but elegant combinations of metal bars, adjusted with due regard to strength and resistance.   Fig. 5.*

There were many fine specimens of this style of railing round tombs, and Westminster Abbey was rich in such examples, but they were actually pulled down and sold for old iron by the order of the then Dean, and even the exquisite scroll-work belonging to the tomb of Queen Eleanor, of which I have here given a specimen (fig. 6), was not respected.   The iron screen of King Edward the Fourth's tomb at St. George's Chapel, Windsor, is a splendid example of ancient iron-work.

The fire-dogs or Andirons (fig. 7), as they were called, which supported either the fuel-logs where wood was burnt, or grates for coal, were frequently of splendid design.   The ornaments were generally heraldic, and

* The parts marked with a + in this figure are merely pierced out of *thin* plate, and riveted to the bars.

it was not unusual to work the finer parts in brass for relief of colour and richness of effect.

These form a striking contrast with the inconsistencies of modern grates, which are not unfrequently made to represent diminutive fronts of castellated or ecclesiastical buildings with turrets, loopholes, windows, and doorways, all in a space of forty inches.

New Sheffield pattern for a modern Castellated Grate.

The fender is a sort of embattled parapet, with a lodge-gate at each end; the end of the poker is a sharp pointed finial; and at the summit of the tongs is a saint. It is impossible to enumerate half the absurdities of modern metal-workers; but all these proceed from the false notion of *disguising* instead of *beautifying* articles of utility. How many objects of ordinary use are rendered monstrous and ridiculous simply because the artist, instead of seeking the *most convenient form*, and *then decorating it*, has embodied some extravagance *to conceal the real purpose for which the article has been made!* If a clock is required, it is not unusual to cast a Roman warrior in a flying chariot, round one of the wheels of which, on close inspection, the hours may be descried; or the whole front of a cathedral church reduced to a few inches in height, with the clock-face

Patterns of Brumagem Gothic.

occupying the position of a magnificent rose window. Surely the inventor of this patent clock-case could never have reflected that according to the scale on which the edifice was reduced, his clock would be about two hundred feet in circumference, and that such a monster of a dial would crush the proportions of almost any building that could be raised. But this is nothing when compared to what we see continually produced from those inexhaustible mines of bad taste, Birmingham and Sheffield: stair-case turrets for inkstands, monumental crosses for light-shades, gable ends hung on handles for door-porters, and four doorways and a cluster of pillars to support a French lamp; while a pair of *pinnacles* supporting an arch is called a Gothic-pattern scraper, and a wiry compound of quatrefoils and fan tracery an abbey garden-seat. Neither relative scale, form, purpose, nor unity of style, is ever considered by those who design these abominations; if they only introduce a quatrefoil or an acute arch, be the outline and style of the article ever so modern and debased, it is at once denominated and sold as Gothic.

While I am on this topic it may not be amiss to mention some other absurdities which may not be out of place, although they do not belong to metal-work. I will commence with what are termed Gothic-pattern papers, for hanging walls, where a wretched caricature of a pointed building is repeated from the skirting to the cornice in glorious confusion,—door over pinnacle, and pinnacle over door. This is a great favourite with hotel and tavern keepers. Again, those papers which are shaded are defective in principle; for, as a paper is hung round a room, the ornament must frequently be shadowed on the light side.

Pattern of Modern Gothic Paper.

The variety of these miserable patterns is quite surprising; and as the expense of cutting a block for a bad figure is equal if not greater than for a good one, there is not the shadow of an excuse for their continual reproduction. A moment's reflection must show the extreme absurdity of *repeating a perspective* over a large surface with some hundred different points of sight: a panel or wall may be enriched and decorated at pleasure, but it should always be treated in a consistent manner.

Flock papers are admirable substitutes for the ancient hangings, but then they must consist of a pattern *without shadow*, with the forms relieved by the introduction of harmonious colours. Illuminated manuscripts of the thirteenth, fourteenth, and fifteenth centuries would furnish an immense number of exquisite designs for this purpose.

Ancient Pattern for a Flock Paper.

These observations will apply to modern carpets, the patterns of which are generally *shaded*. Nothing can be more ridiculous than an apparently *reversed groining* to walk upon, or highly relieved foliage and perforated tracery for the decoration of a floor.

The ancient paving tiles are quite consistent with their purpose, being merely ornamented with a pattern not produced by any apparent relief, but only by *contrast of colour;* and carpets should be treated in precisely the same manner. Turkey carpets, which are by far the handsomest now manufactured, have no shadow in their pattern, but merely an intricate combination of coloured intersections.

Pattern of Ancient Paving Tiles.

Modern upholstery, again, is made a surprising vehicle for bad and paltry taste, especially when any thing very fine is attempted.

To arrange curtains consistently with true taste, their use and intention should always be considered: they are suspended across windows and other openings to exclude cold and wind, and as they are not always required to be drawn, they are hung to rings sliding on rods, to be opened or closed at pleasure: as there must necessarily be a space between this rod and the ceiling through which wind will pass, a boxing of wood has been contrived, in front of which a valance is suspended to exclude air.

Now the materials of these curtains may be rich or plain, they may be heavily or lightly fringed, they may be embroidered with heraldic charges or not, according to the locality where they are to be hung, but their real use must be strictly maintained. Hence all the modern plans of suspending enormous folds of stuff over poles, as if for the purpose of sale or of being dried, is quite contrary to the use and intentions of curtains, and abominable in taste; and the only object that these endless festoons and bunchy tassels can answer is to swell the bills and profits of the upholsterers, who are the inventors of these extravagant and ugly draperies, which are not only useless in protecting the chamber from cold, but are the depositories of thick layers of dust, and in London not unfrequently become the strong-holds of vermin.

ANTIENT CVRTAIN HANGINGS

It is not less ridiculous to see canopies of tomb and altar screens set up

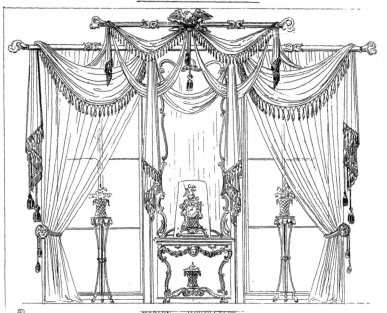

MODERN UPHOLSTERY.

over windows, instead of the appropriate valance or baldaquin of the olden time. It is proper in this place to explain the origin and proper application of fringe, which is but little understood. Fringe was originally nothing more than the ragged edge of the stuff, tied into bunches to prevent it unravelling further. This suggested the idea of manufacturing fringe as an ornamental edging, but good taste requires that it should be both *designed and applied consistently*.

In the first place, fringe should never consist of *heavy parts*, but simply of threads tied into ornamental patterns.

Modern Fringe, composed of turned
pieces of wood.

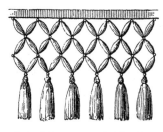

Ancient Fringe, composed of threads.

Secondly, a deep fringe should not be suspended to a narrow valance.

Thirdly, no valance should be formed entirely of fringe, as fringe can only be applied as an ornamental edging to some kind of stuff.

Fourthly, fringe should not be sewed *upon* stuff, but always *on the edges*. It is allowable at the very

A Modern Valance of Fringe.

top, as it may be supposed to be the upper edge turned over.

But to return to metal-work. We have in the next place to consider the use of cast-iron. When viewed with reference to mechanical purposes, it must be considered as a most valuable invention, but it can but rarely be applied to ornamental purposes.

Iron is so much stronger a material than stone that it requires, of course, a much smaller substance to attain equal strength; hence, to be consistent, the mullions of cast-iron tracery must be so reduced as to look painfully thin, devoid of shadow, and out of all proportion to the openings in which they are fixed. If, to overcome these objections, the castings are made of the same dimensions as stone, a great inconsistency with respect to the material is incurred; and, what will be a much more powerful argument with most people, treble the cost of the usual material.

Moreover, all castings must be deficient of that play of light and shade consequent on bold relief and deep sinkings, so essential to produce a good effect.

Cast-iron is likewise a source of continual repetition, subversive of the variety and imagination exhibited in pointed design. A mould for casting is an expensive thing; once got, it must be worked out.

Cast-iron Mullion.   Stone Mullion.

Hence we see the same window in green-house, gate-house, church, and room; the same strawberry-leaf, sometimes perpendicular, sometimes horizontal, sometimes suspended, sometimes on end; although by the principles of pure design these various positions require to be differently treated.

Cast-iron is a deception; it is seldom or never left as iron. It is disguised by paint, either as stone, wood, or marble. This is a mere trick, and the severity of Christian or Pointed Architecture is utterly opposed to all deception: better is it to do a little substantially and consistently with truth than to produce a great but false show. Cheap deceptions of magnificence encourage persons to assume a semblance of decoration far beyond either their means or their station, and it is to this cause we may assign all that mockery of splendour which pervades even the dwellings of the lower classes of society. Glaring, showy, and meretricious ornament was never so much in vogue as at present; it disgraces every branch of our art and manufactures, and the correction of it should be an earnest consideration with every person who desires to see the real principles of art restored.

I will now briefly notice the exquisite productions of the ancient gold and silversmiths. As reformers and puritans have left us nothing but the mere name of the glorious shrines and ornaments which formerly enriched our cathedral and other churches, and as revolutionary and heretical violence has been almost equally destructive on the continent, were it not for a few places which have preserved their ancient treasures, we should be unable to conceive half the art, half the talent, half the exquisite beauties of this class of ecclesiastical ornaments. In the sacristy of Aix-la-Chapelle is a treasury of inestimable value, consisting of shrines, reliquaries, crosses, crowns, ampuls, chalices, pyxes, books of the Holy Gospels, paxes, and enamelled images of silver, all executed during the finest periods of Christian art, the richness of their material being only surpassed by that of their design. To enumerate even a tenth part of these wonderful productions of the goldsmith's art would occupy far too much time for my present purpose; but I will make a few remarks respecting them to illustrate the purpose of my Lecture.

Their construction and execution is decidedly of a *metallic character*. The ornament is produced by *piercing, chasing, engraving, and enamel:* many of the parts were first formed in thin plates of metal, and then shaped by the pliers. Engraving is a style of ornament peculiar to metal. The old goldsmiths were undoubtedly the inventors of our present engraved plates for printing. They increased the effect of the ornamental engravings, by hollowing out the ground in certain parts, and filling it in with coloured enamels. The annexed engraving of an ancient pyx will show the style of

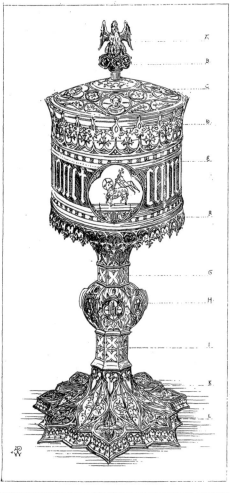

A   The Pelican, chased.

B   The nest, composed of twisted silver wire.

C   Engraved and enamelled.

D   Pierced and engraved.

E   Engraved, and the centre enamelled.

F   Pierced and engraved.

G   Quatrefoils enamelled.

H   Knop beat up with enamelled quatrefoils.

I   Quatrefoils enamelled.

K   Foot hammered up, then engraved and enamelled.

L   Engraved.

working silver, as practised during the middle ages.   There are some exquisite examples of chalice feet enamelled with sacred subjects in the
sacristry of Mayence Cathedral, and a circular reliquary at Aix, which
Dr. Rock considers to have been used as a pax, which is a transcendant
specimen of the art of enamel.   The covers of the great books of the Holy
Gospels were enriched with chasing, enamels, and even jewels ; the crucifixion of our Lord in the centre, and the emblems of the Evangelists at
the corners of an elaborate border.   Precious stones of every description
were studded on these ornaments, which presented a wonderful combination of richness and beauty, produced by gold enamel of various hues
and sparkling gems, arranged with the purest design and most harmonious effect.   As it would occupy a whole work to illustrate these
objects separately, I have endeavoured to convey some idea of their beauty
by the annexed engraving of a reliquary chamber.   Plate V.*

These treasures, which Aix now alone possesses, were by no means
superior to many of those splendid ecclesiastical ornaments formerly to
be found in all the large churches of this land, but which fell a prey
to the rapacious tyrant Henry and his abettors, in the general wreck
of faith and art at the period of his lamentable schism.

Silversmiths are no longer artists ; they manufacture fiddle-headed
spoons, punchy racing cups, cumbersome tureens and wine-coolers ; their
vulgar salvers are covered with sprawling rococo, edged with a confused ·
pattern of such universal use that it may be called with propriety the
Sheffield eternal.   Cruet-stand, tea-pot, candlestick, butter-boat, tray,
waiter, tea-urn, are all bordered with this in and out shell-and-leaf
pattern, which, being struck in a die, does not even possess the merit

---

* REFERENCES TO PLATE V.—I. Ferettum or portable shrine.   II., II. Books of the Holy
Gospels.   III. Relics in a silver bust.   IV. Reliquaries.   V. Relic of the holy cross.   VI.
Paxes for the kiss of peace during the mass.   VII. Morse for fastening a cope.   VIII. Head
of a processional cross.   IX. Precious mitres.   X. Pastoral staff.   XI. Cantor's staff.   XII.
Images of silver gilt.

ALMERY IN A RELIQUARY CHAMBER

Plate V.

London, Published by John Weale, 59, High Holborn, 1841.

of relief. Like every thing else, silver-work has sunk to a mere trade, and art is rigidly excluded from its arrangements.

Iron-smiths were artists formerly, and great artists too; Quentin Matys, for instance, whose beautiful well-top stands in front of Antwerp Cathedral, and whose splendid picture of the entombment of our Lord is the greatest ornament of the Musée of that city. Quentin Matys are not, however, of our generation; if you want some objects executed in iron rather different from what are in ordinary use, and go to a smith to whom you explain your wishes and intentions, the vacant stare of the miserable mechanic soon convinces you that the turning up of a horse-shoe is the extent of his knowledge in the mysteries of the smithy: you then address yourself to another, and one who is called a *capital hand;* and if he be sufficiently sober to comprehend your meaning, he will tell you that what you want is quite out of his line, that he only makes a particular sort of lock, and that he does not think there is a man in the trade who could undertake the job, which, after all, is perhaps a mere copy of a very ordinary piece of old iron-work; and this is a true picture of the majority of our artizans in the nineteenth century, the enlightened age of mechanics' institutes and scientific societies.

Mechanics' institutes are a mere device of the day to poison the minds of the operatives with infidel and radical doctrines; the Church is the true mechanics' institute, the oldest and the best. *She was the great and never failing school in which all the great artists of the days of faith were formed.* Under her guidance they directed the most wonderful efforts of her skill to the glory of God; and let our fervent prayer ever be, that the Church may again, as in days of old, cultivate the talents of her children to the advancement of religion and the welfare of their own souls;—for without such results talents are vain, and the greatest efforts of art sink to the level of an abomination.

LECTURE II.

We will now proceed to consider decoration with regard to constructions in wood, which are founded on quite opposite principles to those of
stone. With timber you may attain a great height, or extend over a
great breadth, by means of a single spar reared on its base or supported
at the ends. The strength of wood-work is attained by bracing the
various pieces together on geometrical principles. This is beautifully
exemplified in ancient roofs, either of churches or domestic buildings :
the construction of these, so far from being concealed, is turned into
ornament. The principal tie-beams, rafters, purloins, and braces, which
in modern edifices are hidden at a vast expense by a flat plaster ceiling,
are here rendered very ornamental features, and this essential portion of
a building becomes its greatest beauty. Plate VI. figs. 1 and 2.

The stupendous roof of Westminster Hall, decidedly the grandest in
the world, illustrates this principle fully, and so do all the roofs in the
collegiate halls of Oxford and Cambridge, as well as those of the palatial
edifices at Eltham, Hampton Court, Croydon, and many others belonging
to manorial residences.

Of wooden roofs over churches we have beautiful specimens in various
parts of England, but especially in Lincolnshire, Norfolk, and Suffolk.
The beams of these roofs are beautifully moulded and enriched with
carvings. Figs. 3, 4.

Nor were these carvings without a mystical and appropriate meaning ;
they usually represented angels, archangels, and various orders of the
heavenly hierarchy, hovering over the congregated faithful, while the
spaces between the rafters were painted azure and powdered with stars
and other celestial emblems, a beautiful figure of the firmament. Some
of these angels held shields charged with the instruments of the passion,
the holy name, and other emblems ; others labels with devout scriptures.
Every portion of these roofs was enriched with painting, and when in
their glory must have formed splendid canopies to the temples of the

ANTIENT ROOF WITH THE FRAMING MADE ORNAMENTAL FIG 1

MODERN ROOF WITH THE FRAMING CONCEALD BY A PLASTERED CEILING FIG 2

BLAKENEY CHURCH NORFOLK FIG 3

BVRY S EDMVNDS FIG 4

Plate VI.

London.Published by John Weale. 59.High Holborn.1841.

living God ; and what is peculiarly useful to illustrate my present purpose, these roofs were of an entirely different construction to coverings of stone. *Wooden groining* is decidedly bad, because it is employing a material *in the place and after the manner of stone, which requires an entirely different mode of construction.*

I am aware that ancient examples of wooden groining are to be found in the cloisters of Lincoln Cathedral, Selby Church, and some others ; but in these cases, as well as any others in which it may be found, an inspection of the building will clearly show that they were originally intended to have been groined with stone, and that the springing ribs have been carried up some height in that material, but that owing to a real or supposed weakness in the side walls, which were not considered capable of resisting the lateral pressure of stone vaulting, the expedient of an imitation groining in wood was resorted to as a case of absolute necessity ; and I am decidedly of opinion that had not the original intention been to have groined these churches in stone, their builders would have made an entirely different arrangement in their upper parts, suitable to an ornamental wooden roof.

At Bury St. Edmund's is a glorious roof, of which I have given a sketch. At every pair of principals are two angels as large as the human figure, bearing the sacred vessels and ornaments used in the celebration of the holy sacrifice ; these angels are vested in chasubles and dalmaticks, tunicles and copes, of ancient and beautiful form ; the candlesticks, thurible, chalice, books, cruets, &c., which they bear are most valuable authorities for the form and design of those used in our ancient churches. The roofs of St. Peter's and All Saints, in that truly catholic city of Norwich, are very fine ; and in Lavenham and Long Melford churches, in Suffolk, are admirable specimens of carved timber roofs.[4]

But, alas ! how many equally fine roofs have been demolished and burnt by the brutal ignorance of parish functionaries !—how many have

---

[4] In the last number of the British Critic is a most admirable article on open roofs, well worthy the perusal of all who are interested in the revival of ancient ecclesiastical architecture.

been daubed over by the remorseless whitewasher!—how many painted in vile imitation of marble, as at Yarmouth, (especially if the church-warden for the time being happened to be a *grainer!*)—how many of these fine roofs have been spoiled of their beautiful and appropriate decorations by the execrable fanaticism of the puritan faction, who actually have made entries in the parish accounts of the cost of their demolition!—how many concealed from view by lath and plaster ceilings of miserable design tacked up under them!—and although a somewhat better spirit has at length arisen, still how many of these beautiful memorials of the piety and skill of our ancestors are yet being mutilated or utterly destroyed under the pretext of reparation!—a plea which is not unfrequently urged by those in authority for selling the lead and massive oak beams, the solid

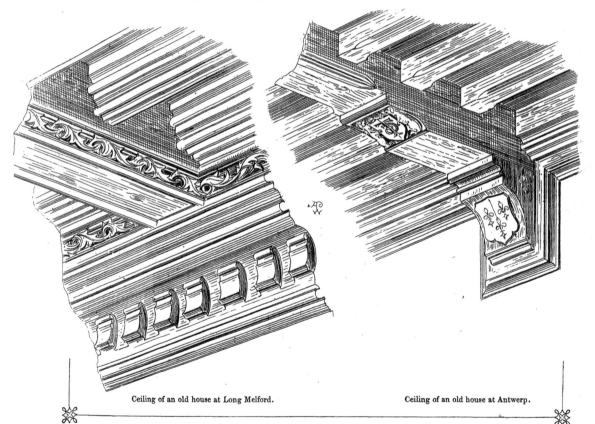

Ceiling of an old house at Long Melford.　　　　Ceiling of an old house at Antwerp.

covering of antiquity, and substituting a plastered ceiling and meagre slates in their stead, which detestable practice is still in full force in many parts of England.

Not only do we find the construction of roofs ornamented, but there are numerous examples of common joist floors and the carrying beams which are rendered exceedingly beautiful by moulding and carving.

Ceiling of the Clopton Chauntry, Long Melford.*

In the ancient timbered houses of which such interesting examples yet remain in many of our old cities, especially at Coventry, York, and Gloucester, we do not *find a single feature introduced beyond the decoration of what was necessary for their substantial construction.* What can be stronger, and at the same time more ornamental, than the curvilineal bracing by which due advantage was taken of crooked pieces of timber!—

* The ground of this ceiling is azure; the stars are of lead, gilt; the inscription on the rafters is 𝕴𝖍𝖚 𝕸𝖊𝖗𝖈𝖞, 𝖆𝖓𝖉 𝕲𝖗𝖆𝖒𝖊𝖗𝖈𝖞; the arms on the shields are those belonging to different branches of the Clopton family, with their names inscribed beneath. The scripture on the large scroll is extracted from the Psalter, the whole richly painted.

The ancient French cities, Rouen, Beauvais, Abbeville, Lisieux, and others, were full of timber houses covered with carved beams and most varied ornaments; but these are rapidly disappearing to make way for monotonous plaster buildings, which are constructed also of *wood;* but as modern architects have not the skill to ornament that construction, the whole of the timbers are

Example of *ornamented construction* in an ancient timber house.

concealed by mock cornices and pilasters, so that the houses of modern

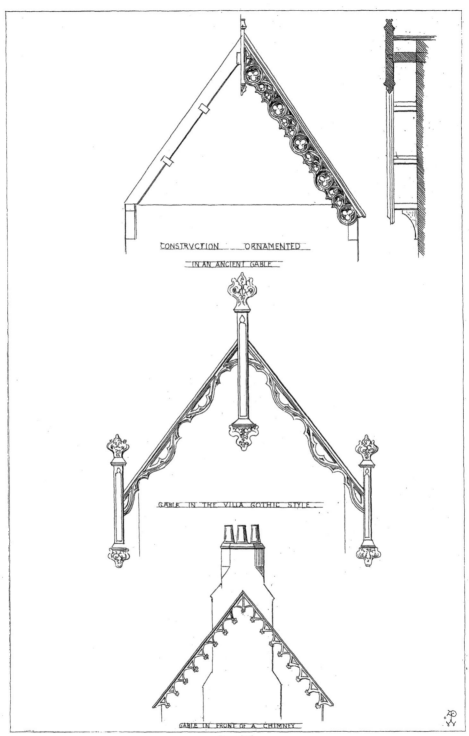

CONSTRUCTION   ORNAMENTED

IN AN ANCIENT GABLE

GABLE IN THE VILLA GOTHIC STYLE

GABLE IN FRONT OF A CHIMNEY

Plate VII.

Rouen have all the disadvantages of the old wooden buildings, without one particle of their beauty.

As gable-ends form most prominent features of the old buildings, and as they are continually attempted by modern Gothic builders, I will draw your attention to their real use, and then point out some of the egregious blunders frequently committed by modern architects when they attempt to introduce them.

The barge boards of gables are intended to cover and preserve the ends of the purloins which projected over to shelter the front of the building.

The hip knop which terminated the ancient gables was in reality a king post fixed at the junction of the barge boards, and into which they were tenanted. To the upper part of these was usually affixed a vane, and the bottom was finished off in the form of a pendant. Plate VII.

In modern gable ends the barge boards are generally so *slight and cut so open* that they become mere skeletons, and utterly useless for the purpose for which they should be fixed, that of covering the timber ends. Again, the knop really useful at the apex of the gable is repeated in modern gables at the extremities, hanging down to an extravagant depth, and loaded with bunchy finials and pendants. Pl. VII.

Of these we may say with Puff in the Critic, when he hears the three morning guns, " Give these fellows a good idea, and they will work it to death." A king post in the centre of the gable is good, because it is really useful, but at the lower extremities these excrescences cannot serve any purpose except to add useless weight and unnecessary expense.

It is a common practice, when a chimney shaft is carried up in the centre of a gable end, for the barge boards *to be fixed before it.* This is absurd; flues must necessarily stop the passage of timbers; consequently the barge boards, which are only coverings of those timbers, should stop also. Pl. VII.

If we examine the ancient wood-work which decorated rooms, we shall
find that it consisted of mere panelling, more or less enriched by carving,
with large spaces left for hangings and tapestry.   Plate VIII.

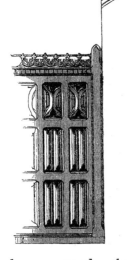

Were the real principles of Gothic architecture
restored, the present objection of its extreme cost-
liness would cease to exist.   In pointed decoration
too much is generally attempted; every room in
what is called a Gothic house must be fitted with
niches, pinnacles, groining, tracery, and tabernacle
work, after the manner of a chantry chapel.   Such
fittings must be enormously expensive, and at the
same time they are contrary to the true spirit of
the style, which does not admit of the introduction
of these features in any situation but that to which
they properly belong.   The modern admirers of
the pointed style have done much injury to its
revival by the erroneous and costly system they
have pursued: the interiors of their houses are one mass of elaborate
work; there is no repose, no solidity, no space left for hangings or
simple panels: the whole is covered with trifling details, enormously
expensive, and at the same time subversive of good effect.   These observations apply equally to furniture;—upholsterers seem to think that
nothing can be Gothic unless it is found in some church.   Hence your
modern man designs a sofa or occasional table from details culled out
of Britton's Cathedrals, and all the ordinary articles of furniture, which
require to be simple and convenient, are made not only very expensive
but very uneasy.   We find diminutive flying buttresses about an arm-
chair; every thing is crocketed with angular projections, innumerable
mitres, sharp ornaments, and turreted extremities.   A man who remains
any length of time in a modern Gothic room, and escapes without being
wounded by some of its minutiæ, may consider himself extremely for-
tunate.   There are often as many pinnacles and gablets about a pier-

Plate VIII.

London, Published by John Weale, 59, High Holborn, 1841.

Illustration of the extravagant style of Modern Gothic Furniture and Decoration.

glass frame as are to be found in an ordinary church, and not unfrequently the whole canopy of a tomb has been transferred for the purpose,
as at Strawberry Hill. I have perpetrated many of these enormities
in the furniture I designed some years ago for Windsor Castle. At
that time I had not the least idea of the principles I am now explaining;
all my knowledge of Pointed Architecture was confined to a tolerably good

notion of details in the abstract; but these I employed with so little judgment or propriety, that, although the parts were correct and exceedingly well executed, collectively they appeared a complete burlesque of pointed design.

I now come, in the last place, to consider decoration with reference to propriety; what I mean by propriety is this, *that the external and internal appearance of an edifice should be illustrative of, and in accordance with, the purpose for which it is destined.* There is a vast difference between a building raised to God and one for temporal purposes; again, in the first of these a great distinction necessarily exists between a cathedral and a parochial church, between a collegiate chapel and a private oratory; and in the second, between a royal residence and a manorial mansion,—between monuments raised for public or national purposes and erections for private convenience.

The scale of propriety in architecture must always be regulated by purpose, and to illustrate this more fully I will divide edifices under three heads,—Ecclesiastical, Collegiate, and Civil. The greatest privilege possessed by man is to be allowed, while on earth, to contribute to the glory of God: a man who builds a church draws down a blessing on himself both for this life and that of the world to come, and likewise imparts under God the means of every blessing to his fellow creatures; hence we cannot feel surprised at the vast number of religious buildings erected by our Catholic forefathers in the days of faith, or at their endeavours to render those structures, by their arrangement and decoration, as suitable as their means could accomplish for their holy and important destination. It must have been an edifying sight to have overlooked some ancient city raised when religion formed a leading impulse in the mind of man, and when the honour and worship of the Author of all good was considered of greater importance than the achievement of the most lucrative commercial speculation. There stood the mother church, the great cathedral, vast in height, rising above all the towers of the parochial churches which surrounded her; next in scale and grandeur might have been discerned the abbatial and collegiate churches with their vast and solemn buildings; each street had its temple raised for the true worship of God, *variously beautiful in design, but each a fine example of Christian art.* Even the bridges and approaches were not destitute of religious buildings, and many a beautiful chapel and oratory was corbelled out on massive piers over the stream that flowed beneath.

The great object I have in directing your attention to such a Catholic city is to illustrate the principle of decorative propriety in ecclesiastical buildings. We have here various edifices of various dimensions, various degrees of richness, various in arrangement, yet each bears on its very face the stamp of Catholic;—cathedral or abbey, church or oratory, they all show that they are dedicated to the one true faith, raised by men actuated by one great motive, the truly Catholic principle of dedicating the best they possessed to God. It would be both unjust and unreasonable to expect a few parishioners to erect as sumptuous an edifice to the Almighty as the clergy of a vast cathedral, and even if they could practically achieve such a result, it would be out of character for the use and intentions of a parish church; neither ought we to look to a private chapel or oratory erected by the unassisted piety of an individual for the extent or ornaments of a public church, unless, indeed, that individual was possessed of great wealth, and then, although not in dimensions, it should surpass in glory the usual decoration of such buildings. In a word, architectural propriety as regards ecclesiastical buildings requires that they should be as good, as spacious, as rich and beautiful, as the *means and numbers of those who are erecting them will permit.* The history of our present vast and magnificent churches fully exemplifies this principle; many of them in their origin were little better than thatched barns; it was the best that could be done at that early period: but when the wealth and influence of the Church increased, they were soon demolished to make way for more fitting structures; these in their turn were rebuilt with still greater magnificence. The ancient clergy were never satisfied, never content, never imagined that they had done enough; the scaffoldings were round the walls and the cranes on the towers of many of the English abbeys at the time of their suppression.

It is not incumbent on all men to raise vast and splendid churches; but it *is* incumbent on all men to render the buildings they raise for religious purposes *more vast and beautiful than those in which they dwell.* This is all I contend for; but this is a feeling nearly, if not altogether, extinct. Churches are now built without the least regard to tradition, to mystical reasons, or even common propriety. A room full of seats at the least possible cost is the present idea of a church; and if any ornament is indulged in, it is a mere screen to catch the eye of the passer-by, which is a most contemptible deception to hide the meanness of the real building. How often do we see a front gable carried up to a respectable pitch, and we might naturally infer that this is the termination, both as regards height and form, of the actual roof; but on turning the corner we soon perceive that it is a mere wall cramped to hold it in its position, and that it conceals a very meeting-house, with a flat roof and low thin walls, perforated by mean apertures, and without a single feature or detail to carry out the appearance it assumed towards the street. Now the

Street Elevation.   Side Perspective.

severity of Christian architecture is opposed to all deception. We should never make a building erected to God appear better than it really is by artificial means. These are showy worldly expedients, adapted only for those who live by splendid deception, such as theatricals, mountebanks, quacks, and the like. Nothing can be more execrable than making a church appear rich and beautiful in the eyes of men, but full of trick and falsehood, which cannot escape the all-searching eye of God, to whom churches should be built, and not to man. Even under the Mosaic dispensation, the Holy of Holies, *entered only by the high priest,* was overlaid with gold; and how much more ought the interiors of our tabernacles to be lined with precious material, which are ten times more holy and deserving of it than the figurative tabernacle of the old law !—and yet in these times all that does not *catch the eye is neglected.* A rich looking antipendium often conceals rough materials, a depository for candle ends, and an accumulation of dirt, which are allowed to remain simply because they are out of sight. All plaster, cast-iron, and composition ornaments, painted like stone or oak, are mere impositions, and, although very suitable to a tea-garden, are utterly unworthy of a sacred edifice. " Omne secundum ordinem et honeste fiat." Let every man build to God according to his means, but not practise showy deceptions; better is it to do a little substantially and consistently with truth, than to produce a great but fictitious effect. Hence the rubble wall and oaken rafter of antiquity yet impress the mind with feelings of reverent awe, which never could be produced by the cement and plaster imitations of elaborate tracery and florid designs which in these times are stuck about mimic churches in disgusting profusion.

It is likewise essential to ecclesiastical propriety that the ornaments introduced about churches should be appropriate and significant, and not consist of *Pagan* emblems and attributes for buildings professedly erected for Christian worship. If the admirers of classic decoration were consistent, on the very principles which induced the ancients to set up their divinities, they should now employ other and more appropriate ornaments; as all those found in the temples and other buildings of the Pagans were in strict accordance with their mythology and customs : *they never intro-*

duced any emblem without a mystical signification being attached to it. Now, great as may be their enormities, I think it would be unjust to charge the advocates of revived Pagan decoration with an actual belief in the mythology of which they are such jealous admirers; hence they are guilty of the greater inconsistency, as the original heathens proceeded from conviction. They would not have placed urns on the tombs, had they not practised burning instead of burying the dead; of which former custom the urn was a fitting emblem, as being the depository for the ashes. Neither would they have decorated the friezes with the heads of sheep and oxen, had they not sacrificed those animals to their supposed gods, or placed inverted torches on the mausoleums, had they believed in the glories of the Resurrection. But what have we, as *Christians*, to do with all those things illustrative *only of former error?* Is our wisdom set forth by the owl of Minerva, or our strength by the club of Hercules? What have we (who have been redeemed by the sacrifice of our Lord Himself) to do with the carcasses of bulls and goats? And how can we

(who surround the biers of our departed brethren with blazing tapers, denoting our hope and faith in the glorious light of the Resurrection,) carve the *inverted torch of Pagan despair* on the very tomb to which we conduct their remains with such sparkling light? Let us away with such gross inconsistencies, and restore the Christian ideas of our Catholic ancestors, for they alone are proper for our imitation. But not only are the

Modern Tomb in the revived Pagan style. details of modern churches borrowed from Pagan instead of Christian antiquity, but the very plan and arrangement of the buildings themselves are now fashioned after a heathen temple; for which unsightly and inappropriate form modern churchmen and architects have abandoned those which are not only illustrative of the great mysteries of the Christian faith, but whose use has been sanctioned by the custom of more than twelve centuries.

I will now give the following distinct reasons why the architecture of the Greek temples cannot be introduced or imitated with propriety by Christians.

1. These temples were erected for an idolatrous worship, and were suited only for the idolatrous rites which were performed in them. 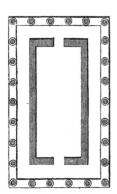 The interior, entered only by the priests, was comparatively small, and either dark or open at top, while the peristyle and porticoes were spacious, for the people who assisted without. There is not the slightest similarity between our worship and the idolatrous worship of the Greeks. We require that the people should be *within* the church, not outside. If, therefore, you adopt a perfect Greek temple, your interior will be confined and ill-suited for the intended purpose, while your exterior will occasion an enormous outlay without any utility. If, on the other hand, you strip a Greek temple of its external peristyle, and build your external walls in the place of the pillars, you entirely destroy the most beautiful feature of the architecture, and the building becomes a miserable departure from the style it professes to imitate.

2. The Greeks did not introduce windows in their temples ; they are essentially necessary with us. Perforate the walls with windows, and you again destroy the simplicity and unity of Greek architecture, which its admirers extol as one of its greatest beauties.

3. Christian churches require bells, by the sound of which the faithful may be called to their devotions. The bells, to be distinctly heard, must be suspended in a tower or belfry, and these are features utterly unknown in Greek architecture. A tower composed of a number of small porticoes, set over one another, and placed in front of a mock

temple, is a most glaring absurdity; nor is a tower of this description, starting out of nothing at the top of a portico, any better. Figs. 1 and 2.

Figure 1.   Figure 2.

4. Our northern climate requires an acute pitch of roof to prevent the accumulation of snow and to resist weather.[5] The Greeks, whose climate is the reverse of ours, had their roofs and pediments exceedingly flat; nor could they be raised to our proper pitch without violating the character of their architecture. Fig. 3.

Fig. 3.

In short, Greek temples are utterly inapplicable to

[5] It is to be remarked that flat-pitched roofs were not introduced into English pointed churches till after the decline of that style, and the marks of the old high gabled roofs are generally to be seen in the towers of those churches where the present roofs are flat, proving them to have been altered subsequent to the original erection of the buildings.

the purpose of Christian churches;[6] and the attempt is little short of madness when our country is literally covered with beautiful models of ecclesiastical structures of every dimension, *the architecture and arrangement of which have originated in their wants and purpose.* An old English parish church, as originally used for the ancient worship, was one of the most beautiful and appropriate buildings that the mind of man could conceive; every portion of it answered both a useful and mystical purpose. There stood the tower, not formed of *detached and misapplied* portions of architectural detail stuck over one another to make up a height, but solid buttresses and walls rising from a massive base, and gradually diminishing and enriching as they rise, till they were terminated in a heaven-pointing spire surrounded by clusters of pinnacles, and forming a beautiful and instructive emblem of a Christian's brightest hopes. These towers served a double purpose, for in them hung the solemn sounding bells to summon the people to the offices of the church, and by their lofty elevation they served as beacons to direct their footsteps to the sacred spot. Then the southern porch, destined

[6] Neither are they better adapted for domestic purposes; for it is still more absurd to see two or three tiers of windows introduced in the shell of a Greek temple, the roof of which is broken by numerous stacks of vainly disguised chimneys. Yet notwithstanding the palpable impracticability of adapting the Greek temples to our climate, habits, and religion, we see the attempt and failure continually made and repeated: post-office, theatre, church, bath, reading-room, hotel, methodist chapel, and turnpike-gate, all present the eternal sameness of a Grecian temple outraged in all its proportions and character.

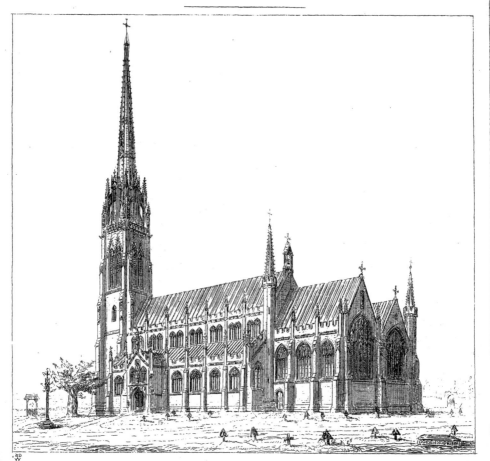

for the performance of many rites,—the spacious nave and aisles for the faithful,—the oaken canopy carved with images of the heavenly host, and painted with quaint and appropriate devices,—the impressive doom or judgment pictured over the great chancel arch,—the fretted screen and rood loft,—the mystical separation between the sacrifice and the people, with the emblem of redemption carried on high and surrounded with glory,—the great altar, rich in hangings, placed far from irreverent gaze, and with the brilliant eastern window terminating this long perspective; while the chantry and guild chapels, pious foundations of families and confraternities, contributed greatly to increase the solemnity of the

A General Prospect of Saint Mary Winton College.

Plate IX.

London. Published by John Weale, 59. High Holborn. 1841.

glorious pile.   Such is but a faint outline of the national edifices which have been abandoned for pewed and galleried assembly rooms, decorated only with gas fittings and stoves, and without so much as one holy or soul-stirring emblem about them.

We will now examine architectural propriety with reference to collegiate architecture.   Our old English Catholic colleges (Plate IX.) will illustrate most beautifully the principle I wish to demonstrate.   The main feature of these buildings was the chapel: to our Catholic forefathers the celebration of the divine office with becoming solemnity and splendour formed a primary consideration, and ample was the provision made for this purpose in all the old collegiate foundations.   The place set apart for this holy purpose generally towered over the surrounding buildings. The chapels of King's College and Eton can be distinctly seen many miles before the subordinate buildings can be discerned.   Oxford, at a distance, presents a complete grove of towers, spires, and pinnacled turrets, rising from the collegiate churches.   After this principal feature, every portion of these edifices had its distinguishing character and elevation: in order to give due effect to the gate-house, refectory, and other important parts of the building, the chambers never exceeded the height of one story above the ground floor.[7]   A very characteristic feature of the old collegiate buildings is the position of the chimneys, which are made to project from the front walls of the buildings.   This, I am well aware, has been considered a defect by ignorant modern artists, but will be found on examination, like all other practices of the ancient architects, to be based on excellent practical reasons.

The advantages of this arrangement are as follow: 1. All the internal

---

[7] In those ancient colleges where these chambers have been raised in modern times, the effect of the original design has been completely ruined, and the new collegiate buildings at St. John's, Cambridge, from their height, have all the appearance of a Gothic warehouse or factory.   This is another instance of the folly of using pointed details without following the spirit of the ancient buildings.

space usually occupied by chimney stacks, and which is very considerable, is gained to the apartments.— 2. The stacks of chimneys thus placed act as buttresses to the wall.—3. The danger of fire consequent on chimney flues passing through the woodwork of the roofs is entirely avoided.—4. A great variety of light and shadow, and a succession of bold features, are gained in the building. It is impossible to conceive any buildings better adapted for collegiate purposes, either as regards arrangement or design, than the two establishments founded by that great and good man, William of Wykeham, at Winchester and Oxford. He had two classes to consider in his foundation at Winchester, the clergy and the students. For the former he provided beautiful cloisters retired from the rest of the edifice, suited for contemplation and devotion; while for the latter he assigned ample space for healthy recreation in bad weather, and level meadows for summer sports. The whole character of these buildings is at once severe, elegant, and scholastic; it is precisely what it should be, as the will of Henry the Sixth specifies of the domestic portion of his college at Cambridge, that it should be built *without too great superfluity of detail or busie moulding;*[8] and on this principle Wykeham designed

---

[8] Notwithstanding the directions contained in this will, where the founder's intentions regarding his collegiate buildings are fully and distinctly expressed, the architect (when the glorious opportunity offered a few years since of fulfilling them to the letter, and erecting a

his building. The external ornaments are few, but admirably selected: an image of our blessed Ladye with our Lord is placed over each gateway, in reference to the college being dedicated to God, under the invocation of his blessed mother, towards whom the good bishop entertained an extraordinary devotion, even from his tender years. The other images on either side of the centre niche are those of the angel Gabriel, and Wykeham himself in a kneeling position.

The interior of the chapel (now wofully disfigured) as left by the founder, must have been glorious in the extreme; it consisted of a choir and ante-chapel, by the side of which rose the bell tower, simple, but elegant and lofty.

The members of the society were buried in the cloisters, and also in the ante-chapel, as their memorials of beautifully engraved brass testify. The intention of these was, doubtless, both to incite the surviving community to pray for their souls' repose, and to remind them continually of the similar fate that would inevitably befall them. How Catholic wisdom and Catholic piety stand conspicuous in all the arrangements of these noble buildings! how great the master mind who planned and executed them, and yet how few are there in these days able to understand or willing to imitate them! Can we conceive a more atrocious scheme to destroy the solemn grandeur of Wykeham's church than to allow such a man as Sir Joshua Reynolds to design a transparency for the western end, and appoint *James Wyatt the destructive* to overturn the ancient features and arrangements, setting up the subsellæ of the stalls as brackets for book-desks, and covering the walls with meagre decorations and Bernasconi Gothic!

Modern collegiate buildings,[9] especially on the continent, are the reverse

truly fine building) was allowed to depart entirely from them, and raise a florid structure, arranged in direct opposition to all old collegiate traditions, and the very decorations of which were misapplied details taken from the original chapel, which had been elaborately enriched by the ancient builders for the purpose of distinguishing its sacred destination from the surrounding erections.

[9] It is impossible to conceive a more uncollegiate looking building than what is called the

of all that I have been describing. In them we look in vain for the solemn quadrangle, the studious cloister, the turreted gate-house, the noble refectory with its oak-beamed roof, the mullioned windows and pinnacled parapet, and lofty tower of the church: not a ghost of these venerable characteristics of a college is to be seen, but generally one uniform mass, unbroken either in outline or in face, undistinguishable from other large buildings which surround it. As to its purpose, it might

be taken for a barrack hospital or asylum. How is it possible to expect that the race of men who proceed from these factories of learning will possess the same feelings as those who anciently went forth from the Catholic structures of Oxford and Winchester! We cannot sufficiently admire our English universities; there is nothing like them existing on the continent, notwithstanding the miserable additions and modernizations which have so greatly disfigured the ancient buildings. There is more Catholic scholastic architecture to be found united at Oxford than in any place I have ever visited. Let us hope and pray that its glories may not exist in vain, but that learned and thinking men may be led to draw a parallel in their minds between the faith of those good souls who founded these noble institutions, and our present degraded and half-infidel condition, by which consideration they may be led back to Catholic unity and faith, in which great works can be alone accomplished, or blessings derived from them.

In the third and last place, we will consider architectural propriety with reference to domestic and civil architecture. Most of the mansions erected at the present day in the Italian or pointed architecture, are either bur-

London University, with its useless dome and portico. It may, however, be urged in its defence that any thing *ecclesiastical or Christian* would be very inappropriate, and that the *Pagan* exterior is much more in character with the intentions and principles of the institution.

lesques or false applications of both these styles. In the first place, what does an Italian house do in England? Is there any similarity between our climate and that of Italy? Not the least. Now I will maintain and prove that climate has always had a large share in the formation of domestic architecture, and the Italian is a good illustration of the truth of this remark. The apertures are small; long colonnades for shade, and the whole building calculated for retreat, and protection from heat; the roofs are flat in pitch, from the absence of heavy snow; and plan and outline are both suited to the climate to which the architecture belongs. But we demand in England the very reverse of all this for comfort. We cannot fortunately import the climate of a country with its architecture, or else we should have the strangest possible combination of temperature and weather; and, within the narrow compass of the Regent's Park, the burning heat of Hindoostan, the freezing temperature of a Swiss mountain, the intolerable warmth of an Italian summer, with occasional spots

of our native temperature. I wonder if these ideas ever occur to those who design Italian gardens on the moorlands of England. Truly it will not be a matter of surprise if some searcher after novelty try to cultivate a jungle for imitation tiger-hunting on some old English estate.

Another objection to Italian architecture is this,—we are not Italians, we are Englishmen. God in his wisdom has implanted a love of nation and country in every man, and we should always cultivate this feeling;—we ought to view the habits and manners of other nations without prejudice, derive improvement from all we observe admirable, but we should never forget our own land. Such is, indeed, the extraordinary amalgamation of architecture, style, and manners now in progress, that were it not for the works of nature which cannot be destroyed, and the glorious works of Christian antiquity which have *not yet* been destroyed, Europe would soon present such sameness as to cease to be interesting. Already a sort of bastard Greek, a nondescript modern style, has ravaged many of the most interesting cities of Europe; replacing the original national buildings with unmeaning lines of plaster fronts, without form, without colour, without interest. How many glorious churches have been destroyed within the last few years (*pour faire une place*) for the occasional exercise of the national guard! where a few stunted trees and a puddle of water in a stone basin, which spouts up occasionally some few feet in height, is all we have to see in exchange for some of the most interesting memorials of ancient piety.

England is rapidly losing its venerable garb; all places are becoming alike; every good old gabled inn is turned into an ugly hotel with a stuccoed portico, and a vulgar coffee-room lined with staring paper, with imitation scagliola columns, composition glass frames, an obsequious cheat of a waiter, and twenty per cent. added to the bill on the score of the modern and elegant arrangements. Our good old St. Martin's, St. John's, St. Peter's, and St. Mary's streets, are becoming Belle-vue Places, Adelaide Rows, Apollo Terraces, Regent Squares, and Royal Circuses. Factory chimneys disfigure our most beautiful vales; Government preaching-houses, called churches, start up at the cost of a few hundreds each, by the side of Zion chapels, Bethel Meetings, New Connexions, and Socialist Halls. Timbered fronts of curious and ingenious design are swept away before the resistless torrent of Roman-cement men, who buy their ornaments by

the yard, and their capitals by the ton. Every linen-draper's shop apes to

be something after the palace of the Cæsars; the mock stone columns are fixed over a front of plate glass to exhibit the astonishing bargains; while low-ticketed goods are hung out over the trophies of war. But this is not all; every paltry town has a cigar divan, with something stuck out to look Turkish, and not unfrequently a back parlour travestied into a vile burlesque of eastern architecture. In short, national feelings and national architecture are at so low an ebb, that it becomes an absolute duty in every Englishman to attempt their revival. Our ancient architecture can alone fur-

nish us with the means of doing this successfully; but, unfortunately, those who profess to admire pointed architecture, and who strive to imitate it, produce more ridiculous results than those who fly to foreign aid. What can be more absurd than houses built in what is termed the castellated style? Castellated architecture originated in the wants consequent on a certain state of society: of course the necessity of great strength, and the means of defence suited to the military tactics of the day, dictated to the builders of ancient castles the most appropriate

Modern Castellated Mansion.

style for their construction. Viewed as historical monuments, they are of surprising interest, but as models for our imitation they are worse than useless. What absurdities, what anomalies, what utter contradictions do not the builders of modern castles perpetrate! How many portcullises which will not lower down, and drawbridges which will not draw up!—how many loop-holes in turrets so small that the most diminutive sweep could not ascend them!—On one side of the house machicolated parapets, embrasures, bastions, and all the show of strong defence, and round the corner of the building a conservatory leading to the principal rooms, through which a whole company of horsemen might penetrate at one smash into the very heart of the mansion!—for who would hammer against nailed portals when he could kick his way through the green-house? In buildings of this sort, so far from the turrets being erected for any particular purpose, it is difficult to assign any destination to them after they are erected, and those which are not made into *chimneys* seldom get other occupants than the rooks. But the exterior is not the least inconsistent portion of the edifices, for we find guard-rooms without either weapons or guards; sally-ports, out of which nobody passes but the servants, and where a military man never did go out; donjon keeps, which are nothing but drawing-rooms, boudoirs, and elegant apartments; watch-towers, where the housemaids sleep, and a bastion in which the butler cleans his plate: all is a mere mask, and the whole building an ill-conceived lie.

We will now turn to those mansions erected in what is termed the Abbey style, which are not more consistent than the buildings I have just described. To this class Fonthill belonged, now a heap of ruins, and modern ruins, too, of mere brick and plaster. In such a house something of an ecclesiastical exterior had been obtained at an enormous expense, and a casual passer-by might have supposed from some distance that the place really belonged to some religious community; but on a nearer approach the illusion is soon dissipated, and the building, which had been raised somewhat in the guise of the solemn architecture of religion and antiquity, discovers itself to be a mere toy, built to suit the caprice of a wealthy individual, and devoted to luxury. The seemingly abbey-gate turns out a modern hall, with liveried footmen in lieu of a con-ventual porter; the apparent church nave is only a vestibule; the tower, a lantern staircase; the transepts are drawing-rooms; the cloisters, a furnished passage; the oratory, a lady's boudoir; the chapter-house, a dining-room; *the kitchens alone* are real; every thing else is a deception. Articles of fashionable luxury, glasses in profusion, couches and ottomans, fill the chambers of the mock convent, from whence a prayer never ascends or into which a religious man never enters;—all, in fine, is a mockery and thing of fashion, transient and perishable as the life of its possessor; and if the structure be substantial enough to last his time, it soon after becomes the subject of some auctioneer's puff: its walls are covered with placards; brokers divide the moveables; the whole falls to decay, and is soon only mentioned as a splendid folly.

The old English Catholic mansions were the very reverse of those I have been describing; they were substantial appropriate edifices, suited by

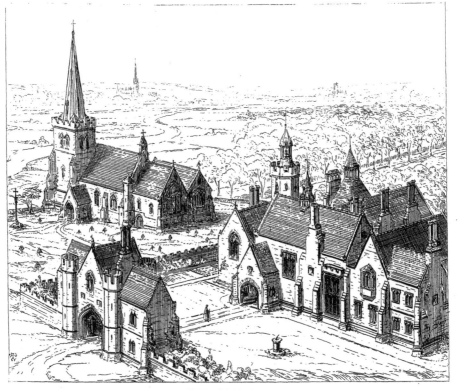

Old English Mansion.

their scale and arrangement for the purposes of habitation. Each part of these buildings indicated its particular destination: the turreted gate-house and porter's lodging, the entrance porch, the high-crested roof and

Louvred hall, with its capacious chimney, the guest chambers, the vast kitchens and offices, all formed distinct and beautiful features, not *masked or concealed under one monotonous front*, but by their variety in form and outline increasing the effect of the building, and presenting a standing illustration of good old English hospitality; while the venerable parish church in the immediate vicinity, with its grey spire and family chantry, showed that the care spiritual was not neglected by our ancestors in the erection of their temporal dwellings.

Every person should be lodged as becomes his station and dignity, for in this there is nothing contrary to, but in accordance with, the Catholic principle; but the mansions erected by our ancestors were not the passing whim of a moment, or mere show places raised at such an extravagant cost as impoverished some generations of heirs to the estates, but solid, dignified, and Christian structures, built with due regard to the general prosperity of the family; and the almost constant residence of the ancient gentry on their estates rendered it indispensable for them to have mansions where they might exercise the rights of hospitality to their fullest extent. They did not confine their guests, as at present, to a few fashionables who condescend to pass away a few days occasionally in a country house; but under the oaken rafters of their capacious halls the lords of the manor used to assemble all their friends and tenants at those successive periods when the church bids all her children rejoice, while humbler guests partook of their share of bounty dealt to them by the hand of the almoner beneath the groined entrance of the gate-house. Catholic England was merry England, at least for the humbler classes; and the architecture was in keeping with the faith and manners of the times,—at once strong and hospitable. There is a great reviving taste for ancient domestic architecture, but a vast many pretended admirers of old English beauties, instead of imitating the Tudor period, when domestic architecture was carried to a high state of perfection, stop short at the reign of Elizabeth, the very worst kind of English architecture; and, strange to say, these unmeaning conglomerations of debased forms have been classed into a regular style, and called after the female tyrant during whose reign they were executed. The only reason I can assign for the fashionable rage for this architecture (if so it may be called) is, that its character is so corrupt, mixed, and bad, that the anachronisms and anomalies so frequently perpetrated by modern architects are made to pass muster under the general term of Elizabethan ; and certainly I cannot deny that the appellation is very appropriate when applied to corrupted design and decayed taste.

I must here mention two great defects very common in modern pointed buildings, both of which arise from the great fundamental principle of decorating utility not being understood. In the first place, many architects apply the details and minor features of the pointed style to classic *masses* and arrangements ; they adhere scrupulously to the regularity and symmetry of the latter, while they attempt to disguise it by the mouldings and accessories of the former. They must have two of every thing, one on each side : no matter if all the required accommodation is contained in one half of the design, a shell of another half must be built to keep up uniformity. What can be more absurd ? Because a man has a real door to enter his house by on one side, he must have a mock one through which he cannot get in on the other. How inconsistent is it to make and glaze a window which is to be *walled up* ab initio ! But to see the full absurdity of this system, let us only imagine the builders of the ancient colleges, after having finished a church and refectory on one side of a quadrangle, running up something to repeat them by way of a pendant on the other, so as to appear two churches and two dining-halls to one college. In the second place, when modern architects avoid this defect of regularity, they frequently fall into one equally great with regard to irregularity ; I mean when a building is *designed to be picturesque*, by sticking as many ins and outs, ups and downs, about it as possible. *The picturesque effect of the ancient buildings results from the ingenious methods by which the old builders overcame local and constructive difficulties.* An edifice which is arranged with the principal view of looking picturesque is sure to resemble an artificial waterfall or a made-up rock, which are generally so *unnaturally natural* as to appear ridiculous.

An architect should exhibit his skill by turning the difficulties which occur in raising an elevation from *a convenient plan* into so many *picturesque beauties;* and this constitutes the great difference between the principles of classic and pointed domestic architecture. In the former *he would be compelled to devise expedients to conceal these irregularities;* in the latter *he has only to beautify them.* But I am quite assured that all the irregularities that are so beautiful in ancient architecture are the result of certain necessary difficulties, and were never purposely designed; for to make a building inconvenient for the sake of obtaining irregularity would be scarcely less ridiculous than preparing working drawings for a new ruin. But all these inconsistencies have arisen from this great error,—*the plans of buildings are designed to suit the elevation, instead of the elevation being made subservient to the plan.*

Under the head of architectural propriety we have also to consider the scale and proportions of buildings. Without vastness of dimensions it is impossible to produce a grand and imposing effect in architecture; still, unless these be regulated on true principles, they may destroy their effect by their very size; and here I wish to draw your attention to a point which will prove the great superiority of the Christian architecture of the middle ages over that of classic antiquity, or of the revived pagan style. In pointed architecture the different details of the edifice are *multiplied with the increased scale of the building:* in classic architecture they are *only magnified.*

To explain this more fully, if the pointed architects had a buttress and pinnacle to erect against some vast structure, such as the Cathedral of Cologne or Amiens, they did not merely increase its dimensions by gigantic water tables, enormous crockets, and a ponderous finial. No! they subdivided it into a *cluster* of piers and pinnacles; they panelled the front, enriched it by subordinate divisions, and by these means the pinnacles of Cologne

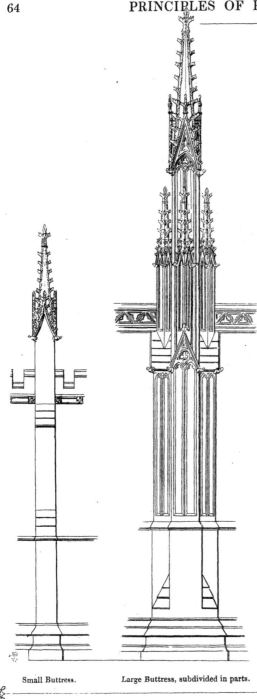

appear five times as large as those of an ordinary church,[10] which could never have been the case had they only *enlarged the scale instead of multiplying the parts*. But the very reverse of this is the case in classic architecture; a column or cornice is the same, *great or small*, whether they are employed in front of an ordinary house or of a vast temple; no distinction except that of size is ever made;

[10] A pillar in classic architecture is a mere cylinder, of large or small diameter. In the pointed style a pillar is subdivided into shafts, which increase in number with its size, and form beautiful clusters.

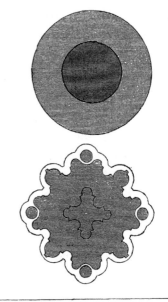

Small Buttress.   Large Buttress, subdivided in parts.

there are the *same number of diameters*, the *same number of mouldings*, the *same relative projections;*—it is merely a *magnifying power* applied to architecture. What is the result? Till you actually stand under these buildings, and find that your chin does not come up to the plinth of the base, you do not perceive the scale. This is perfectly exemplified at St. Peter's. The effect on all who first enter it is that of disappointment; it does not appear any thing like so large as they anticipated. Some of its admirers have tried to pass this off as a great beauty, and have attributed it to its beautiful proportion. This reasoning will not, however, stand the test of close examination; it is essentially false. One of the great arts of architecture is to render a building more vast and lofty in appearance than it is in reality. The contrary effect produced by St. Peter's is not the least among its many defects, and it is purely owing to the *magnifying* instead of the *multiplying principle* having been followed. The great size of its various parts and mouldings required the introduction of colossal figures, which are certain to reduce the appearance of size in any buildings where they are used.

The human figure is a general standard for scale. We are accustomed to assimilate the idea of about five feet nine inches with the height of a man. Hence, be a drawing ever so small, by inserting a diminutive human figure it will immediately convey an idea of the intended size; and on the contrary, if the figures in a drawing be over large, the apparent space represented is immediately reduced in appearance. So is it in architecture: a figure of eighteen feet high will reduce one hundred feet to less than forty in appearance; and the mystery of the disappointing effect of scale in St. Peter's is satisfactorily accounted for. It is all very well for guides and valets de place to astonish travellers by stating that three persons may sit on the great toe of a statue, or that if a figure were laid on its back five men might straddle across the nose; *so much the worse for the effect of the building where such a figure is placed.*

In pointed architecture we seldom find any images larger than the human size, and generally much less. Hence the surprising effect of height and scale conveyed by many old Catholic buildings, which are not in reality half the size of some of their more modern and semi-pagan rivals at Rome.

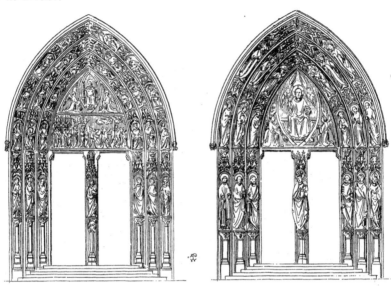

Illustration of the different effects of scale produced by large or small statues in the same space.

In general our English churches are deficient in internal height; not that our national style of Christian art does not possess some fine specimens of this important feature, as in the glorious church of St. Peter, Westminster; but I think the internal vastness of Amiens, Beauvais, Chartres, and others of the French churches, should serve as useful examples to us in this respect in the revival of Pointed and Christian architecture in England. Nothing can be conceived more majestic than those successions of arches divided by light and elegant clusters of shafts running up to an amazing height, and then branching over into beautiful intersected ribs, suspending a canopy of stone at the enormous height of not unfrequently one hundred and fifty feet. Internal altitude is a feature which would add greatly to the effect of many of our fine English churches, and I shall ever advocate its introduction, as it is a characteristic of foreign pointed architecture of which we can avail ourselves without violating the principles of our own peculiar style of English Christian architecture, from which I would not depart in this country on any account. I once stood on the very edge of a precipice in this respect, from which I was rescued by the advice and arguments of my respected and revered friend Dr. Rock, to whose learned researches and observations on Christian antiquities I am highly indebted, and to whom I feel it a bounden duty to make this public acknowledgment of the great benefit I have received from his advice. Captivated by the beauties of foreign pointed architecture, I was on the verge of departing from the severity of our English style, and engrafting portions of foreign detail and arrangement. This I feel convinced would have been a failure ; for although the great principles of Christian architecture were every where the same, each country had some peculiar manner of developing them, and we should continue working in the same parallel lines, all contributing to the grand whole of Catholic art, but by the very variety increasing its beauties and its interest.

In conclusion, Christian verity compels me to acknowledge that there are hardly any defects which I have pointed out to you in the course of this Lecture which could not with propriety be illustrated by my own productions at some period of my professional career. Truth is only gradually developed in the mind, and is the result of long experience and deep investigation. Having, as I conceive, discovered the true principles of pointed architecture, I am anxious to explain to others the errors and misconceptions into which I have fallen, that they, profiting by my experience, may henceforward strive to revive the glorious works of Christian art in all the ancient and *consistent* principles. Let then the Beautiful and the True be our watchword for future exertions in the overthrow of modern paltry taste and paganism, and the revival of Catholic art and dignity.

Laus Deo !

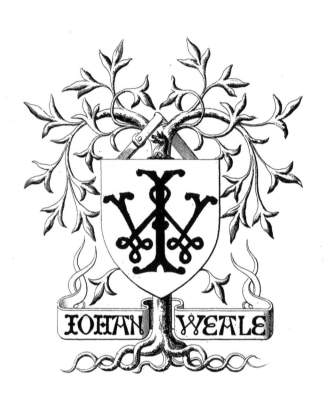

IOHAN WEALE

AN APOLOGY

FOR

The Revival of Christian Architecture.

𝕷𝖔𝖓𝖉𝖔𝖓:

PRINTED BY W. HUGHES, KING'S HEAD COURT, GOUGH SQUARE.

IN THE PRESENT REVIVAL OF CHRISTIAN ARCHITECTURE.

AN APOLOGY

FOR

The Revival of Christian Architecture

IN

ENGLAND.

BY

A. WELBY PUGIN,

ARCHITECT,

PROFESSOR OF ECCLESIASTICAL ANTIQUITIES AT ST. MARIE'S COLLEGE, OSCOTT.

LONDON: JOHN WEALE.

M.CCM.XLIII.

To the Right Honourable

The Earl of Shrewsbury, Waterford, and Wexford.

My very good Lord,

It would be most unnatural and ungrateful in me, when putting forth a Treatise relating to the Revival of Christian Architecture in England, were I not to dedicate the same in an especial manner to your Lordship, who has been the main support in the furtherance of that good work, and to whom I am so greatly bounden.

May God in his mercy grant, that as your Lordship's noble ancestor, the Talbot of famous memory, extended the temporal glory of England by deeds of arms, so may your Lordship continue to increase the spiritual welfare of these realms by reviving the ancient glories of the English Church, of whose faith your noble house has furnished so many witnesses.

That your Lordship may long be blessed with health and strength to carry out to a happy conclusion the many good designs you have in hand, is the constant prayer of

Your Lordship's devoted and faithful Bedesman,

✝ A. Welby Pugin.

LIST OF PLATES.

REFERENCES TO THE FRONTISPIECE.

1. St. George's, London.
2. St. Peter's, Woolwich.
3. St. Marie's, Stockton.
4. St. Giles's, Cheadle.
5. St. Marie's, Newcastle-on-Tyne.
6. North Gate, St. Marie's, Oscott.
7. St. Austin's, Kenilworth.
8. Jesus Chapel, Pomfret.
9. Cathedral, Killarney.
10. St. Chad's, Birmingham.
11. St. Oswald's, Liverpool.
12. Holy Cross, Kirkham.
13. St. Barnabas, Nottingham.
14. Gorey, Ireland.
15. St. Marie's, Derby.
16. St. Alban's, Macclesfield.
17. St. Marie's, Brewood.
18. St. Winifride's, Shepshead.
19. St. Andrew's, Cambridge.
20. St. Bernard's Priory, Leicestershire.
21. St. Marie's, Keighley.
22. St. Marie's, Warwick Bridge.
23. St. Wilfrid's, Manchester.
24. St. Marie's, Southport.
25. St. John's Hospital, Alton.

AN APOLOGY

FOR

THE REVIVAL OF CHRISTIAN ARCHITECTURE
IN ENGLAND.

THE age in which we live is a most eventful period for English art. We are just emerging from a state which may be termed the dark ages of architecture. After a gradual decay of four centuries, the style,—for style there was,—became so execrably bad, that the cup of degradation was filled to the brim; and as taste had fallen to its lowest depth, a favourable re-action commenced.

The breaking up of this wretched state of things has naturally produced a complete convulsion in the whole system of arts, and a Babel of confusion has succeeded to the one bad idea that generally prevailed.

Private judgment runs riot; every architect has a theory of his own, a beau ideal he has himself created; a disguise with which to invest the building he erects. This is generally the result of his latest travels. One breathes nothing but the Alhambra,—another the Parthenon,— a third is full of lotus cups and pyramids from the banks of the Nile,—a fourth, from Rome, is all dome and basilica; whilst another works Stuart and Revett on a modified plan, and builds lodges, centenary chapels, reading-rooms, and fish-markets, with small Doric work and white brick facings. Styles are now *adopted* instead of *generated*, and ornament and design *adapted to*, instead of *originated by*, the edifices themselves.

This may, indeed, be appropriately termed the *carnival* of architecture: its professors appear tricked out in the guises of all centuries and all nations; the Turk and the Christian, the Egyptian and the Greek, the Swiss and the Hindoo, march side by side, and mingle together; and some of these gentlemen, not satisfied with perpetrating one character, appear in two or three costumes in the same evening.[1]

Amid this motley group (oh! miserable degradation!) the venerable form and sacred detail of our national and Catholic architecture may be discerned; but *how* adopted? Not on consistent principle, not on authority, not as the expression of our faith, our government, or country, but as one of the disguises of the day, to be put on and off at pleasure, and used occasionally as circumstances or private caprice may suggest.

It is considered suitable for some purposes,—MELANCHOLY, and *therefore fit for religious* buildings!!! a style that an architect of the day should be acquainted with, in order to please those who admire old things,[2]—a style in which there are many beauties: such is the heartless advocacy which our national architecture frequently receives from its professed admirers; while others are not wanting, even in the most influential positions, who venture to sneer at and insult its principles, either because they are far beyond their comprehension, or that they

---

[1] It is not unusual for architects to send two designs for the same building, of utterly opposed character and style, for the selection of the committee; as if it were possible for more than one principle to be a correct expression of the intended building.

[2] If a pointed design is sent, it is generally in accordance with the whim of the architect's employer; and then a symmetrical front regular, to the utter inconvenience of the internal arrangements, is dressed up with tracery, battlements, and pinnacles; and these sit as uneasy on the modern block, as the chimney stacks and attics on an Albert Terrace Parthenon.

are so besotted in their mongrel compositions, that they tremble at the ascendancy of truth.[3]

The object of this tract is, therefore, to place Christian architecture

---

[3] It is a perfect disgrace to the Royal Academy, that its Professor of Architecture should be permitted to poison the minds of the students of that establishment by propagating his erroneous opinions of Christian architecture. The influence which his position naturally gives him over their minds is doubtless considerable, and the effect of his instructions proportionably pernicious. Not content, however, with the disparagement of ancient excellence, which he introduces in his official lectures, he is *practically* carrying out his contempt of pointed design in both Universities, and in a manner that must cause anguish of soul to any man of Catholic mind and feeling.

The ancient buildings of King's College, models of perfection in their way, are actually being demolished, to make room for a monstrous erection of mongrel Italian, a heavy, vulgar, unsightly mass, which already obscures from some points the lateral elevation of King's Chapel, and which it is impossible to pass without a depression of spirits and feelings of disgust. A man who paganizes *in the Universities* deserves no quarter; and it becomes a question whether the greater share of blame attaching to such transactions is due to the architect who could so wed himself to the bastard compositions generated in his studio, as to intrude his huge deformity not only in the vicinity but on the site of ancient excellence; or to the authorities of the University, who, in the very teeth of the present revival, have sanctioned so gross a violation of propriety. But their madness is paralleled at Oxford, where the same architect is erecting another unsightly pile of pagan details, stuck together to make up a show, for the university galleries immediately facing the venerable front of St. John's, and utterly destroying this beautiful entrance to the most Catholic-looking city in England. The pagan character of this edifice has, however, awakened the disgust of some of the most learned members of the University; and if it pleases the admirers of gin-palace design, it will draw down the indignation of every true disciple of Catholic and consistent architecture.

But, although some men, by dint of name, fortune, and station, may rule for a brief space, and mock that excellence to which they can never attain, yet their day is fast drawing to a close;—several of the junta who have disfigured the face of the country are already gone; and, like Bunyan's giants in the Pilgrim's Progress, the others are so enfeebled that they can only snarl at the revival of excellence. Their works will hardly be endured for the time they have to run, and the remembrance of them will be the laughing-stock of posterity; and when the ancient glories of our native land are restored, and this generation of pretenders have passed away, men will be amazed that a period could have existed when they were permitted to disfigure and destroy, unchecked and unreproved.

in its true position,—to exhibit the claims it possesses on our veneration and obedience, as the only correct expression of the faith, wants, and climate of our country; and if it fails in doing this, it will be rather owing to the incapacity of the author in doing justice to this most important subject, than to any want of truth in the proposition itself.

The arguments used, both by the advocates and opponents of pointed architecture, have been most fallacious. They have consisted, for the most part, in mere private views and opinions relative to comparative abstract beauty in the different styles; and these, as might be expected, have proved most inconclusive.

To advocate Christian architecture merely on the score of its beauty, can never prevail with those, who profess to think that all art and majesty is concentrated in a Grecian temple. We must turn to the principles from which all styles have originated. The history of architecture is the history of the world: as we inspect the edifices of antiquity, its nations, its dynasties, its religions, are all brought before us. The belief and manners of all people are embodied in the edifices they raised; it was impossible for any of them to have built consistently otherwise than they did: each was the inventor and perfecter of their peculiar style; each style was the type of their Religion, customs, and climate. The abstract beauty of these various styles, when viewed with reference to the purposes for which they were raised, is great indeed; they are the perfection of what was intended: a follower of Bramah or Isis, a fire-worshipper of Persia, could not have produced any thing different from what they have done; and so truly did these edifices embody the principles and worship of their builders, that the discovery of a certain form of temple or peculiar symbols is at once admitted as evidence, of the existence of a certain people and religion in that place. Nay, more, by architecture and ornament alone, learned men of the present time are enabled to make the most important discoveries, relative to the history of nations, whose very existence is anterior by many centuries to the Christian era.

Will the architecture of our times, even supposing it solid enough to last, hand down to posterity any certain clue or guide to the system under which it was erected? Surely not; it is not the expression of existing opinions and circumstances, but a confused jumble of styles and symbols borrowed from all nations and periods.

Are not the adapters of pagan architecture violating every principle, that regulated the men whose works they profess to imitate? These uncompromising advocates of classic styles would be utterly repudiated by the humblest architect of pagan antiquity, were he now to return to earth. Vitruvius would spew if he beheld the works of those who glory in calling him master.

The restorers of Christian architecture are more consistent followers of classic *principles* than all these boasted Greeks; they understand antiquity, and apply the ancient consistent rules to the new dispensation. The moderns, in their pretended imitation of the classic system, are constantly producing the greatest anomalies; and we are called upon to admire their thrice-cooked hashes of pagan fragments (in which the ingredients are amalgamated in utter confusion) as fine national monuments of the present age.

I have not unfrequently been denominated by the perpetrators of these absurdities as a fanatic for pointed design, a blind bigot insensible to, and ignorant of, any beauty but that of the middle ages. So far from this, I much question, if I am not better acquainted with the principles on which the various styles of pagan antiquity were founded, than many of their warmest advocates. I believe them to be the *perfect expressions* of *imperfect systems;* the summit of human skill, expended on human inventions: but I claim for Christian art a merit and perfection, which it was impossible to attain even in the Mosaic dispensation, much less in the errors of polytheism. The former was but a type of the great blessings we enjoy,—the latter, the very antipodes to truth, and the worship of demons.

I can readily understand how the pyramid, the obelisk, the temple, and pagoda have arisen; whence the arrangement of their plan, and the symbols which decorate them have been generated. I am prepared to join in admiration at the skill which piled such gigantic masses on each other, which fashioned so exquisitely each limb and countenance; but I cannot acknowledge them to be appropriate types for the architecture of a Christian country.

If we worshipped Jupiter, or were votaries of Juggernaut, we should raise a temple, or erect a pagoda. If we believed in Mahomet, we should mount the crescent, and raise a mosque. If we burnt our dead, and offered animals to gods, we should use cinerary urns, and carve sacrificial friezes of bulls and goats. If we denied Christ, we should reject his Cross. For all these would be natural consequences: but, in the name of common sense, whilst we profess the creed of Christians, whilst we glory in being Englishmen, let us have an architecture, the arrangement and details of which will alike remind us of our faith and our country, —an architecture whose beauties we may claim as our own, whose symbols have originated in our religion and our customs. Such an architecture is to be found in the works of our great ancestors, whose noble conceptions and mighty works were originated and perfected under a faith and system, for the most part common with our own; for, strange as it may appear, the difference between us and our English forefathers, on examination, will prove slight indeed, compared with those nations, from whom we have been accustomed for the last century to borrow our types, as being the best suited to our present habits.

Before entering into the necessary details in support of this position, it may not be amiss to say a few words on the subject of Christian architecture. It has been frequently objected by the advocates of paganism, that the pointed style, especially Christian, was not developed till several centuries after the crucifixion of our Lord; but this is measuring the ways of God by mere human capacity. How long were the chosen people of God allowed to exist before the erection of the great temple of Jerusalem was permitted? Did not the skins of the desert typify the polished stones of that wondrous structure? And may we not say that the foundations of Cologne were commenced in the catacombs of the eternal city? Like protestants who rail at ecclesiastical solemnity, because it is not to be found in the persecuted church of the apostles, they urge the non-existence of spires under Roman emperors as a proof, that they were not generated by the Christian principle. But modern men are constantly referring to the church in her suffering state, described by our Lord under the similitude of a grain of mustard-seed, while they refuse to recognise her, when, as the greatest of all trees, she extended triumphant in beauty and luxuriant foliage over the earth.

How could the divine character of Christ's church have been made manifest to future generations, except by passing through an ordeal of poverty and bitter persecution of more than three centuries, and triumphing over the powers of the world and darkness, without human aid! Those were not, indeed, times for the cultivation of material arts; but the foundations of every Christian temple, spire, and pinnacle, were then laid so firmly, that we may build on them till doomsday without fear of sinking or decay. Byzantine, Lombard, Saxon, and Norman, were all various developements of Christian architecture on a cruciform plan with Christian symbols. Pointed architecture was the crowning result of these earlier efforts, which may be considered as the centering on which the great arch was turned.

The change which took place in the sixteenth century was not a matter of mere taste, but a change of soul; it was a great contention between Christian and pagan ideas, in which the latter triumphed, and for the first time *inconsistency* in architectural design was developed. Previous to that period, architecture had always been a correct type of the various systems, in which it was employed; but, from the moment the Christians adopted this fatal mistake, of reviving classic design, the principles of architecture have been plunged into miserable confusion. The gradual developement of inconsistent design is exceedingly curious.

At first it was confined to the substitution of a bastard sort of Italian detail to the ancient masses. This is particularly striking in the French buildings erected during the reign of Francis the First, where the high-pitched roofs, lofty turrets and chimney stacks, cresting buttresses, string courses, mullions, and all the natural and consistent features of ancient design, are retained with pagan capitals, friezes, and arabesques.[4] The church of St. Eustache, at Paris, is a most remarkable example of this period. It is perfectly Christian in its plan and arrangement, being cruciform, with double aisles and lateral chapels, a grand apsis and lady chapel, triforium, clerestory, pinnacles, flying buttresses, immense height, and all the features of a noble pointed church; but with debased Roman mouldings, cornices, and details, the very canopies over the images being composed of small pediments and domes. Thus, although the builders of the so-called *renaissance* opened the flood-gates of innovation, they had not lost *natural composition;* they only decorated what they required in an inconsistent manner: but the temple and regularity system had not come in. Indeed, we shall find that, down to the last century, many of the old principles were retained in both domestic and ecclesiastical buildings;[5] and it is only within a comparatively short time that error and inconsistency has attained its climax, by flattening and concealing roofs, disguising chimney stacks, building sham windows, compoing over brick walls, and dressing up Italian masses with pointed details, gathered from all styles, dates, and buildings.

---

[4] See Plate II.

[5] In several of the manor-houses erected during the seventeenth century, the chimney stacks are not concealed but ornamented, while the high roofs, gable ends, bay windows, turrets, and consistent features of the old domestic architecture, are all retained.

Wadham College, and the chapel of Brazennose, at Oxford, and the chapel of Peterhouse, Cambridge, may also be cited as illustrations of this fact.

Even in some of the older squares in London, such as Red Lion and Queen's, the houses had high roofs, with bold overhanging cornices and good dormer windows. Near New Street, Fetter Lane, some houses of this character are yet remaining, and are infinitely superior to the street erections of the present time.

✠ WEST FRONT CHVRCH OF CISORS 16 CENT.   GATEWAY CHATEAV GAILLON 16 CENT.

EXAMPLES OF THE INTRODVCTION OF PAGAN DETAILS WITH THE ANTIENT MASSES IN THE 16 CENT.

Never, in the annals of architecture, have so many glorious opportunities offered, in a short space of time, for the accomplishment of noble buildings. Within my own recollection, three royal palaces, half the metropolis, churches without number, vast restorations, entire colleges in both universities, galleries, civic buildings, bridges, hospitals, houses, public monuments, in every possible variety; and, with the exception of the New Houses of Parliament, we have not one edifice of the whole number that it is not painful to contemplate as a monument of national art. Every chance has been fairly thrown away, as it offered: of money, there has been an ample supply; for the cost of the various works has been something *enormous*; in all cases sufficient to have produced a good thing, and in many instances far more than was required. Now the cause of all these failures is the same, and may be summed up in three words, *inconsistency of design.* In no one instance has the purpose or destination of the building formed the ground-work of the composition: Grecian or Gothic, Ecclesiastical or Civil, it has been a mere system of *adaptation.* One man has adapted a temple, another a castle, a third an abbey; but temples, castles, and abbeys owed their existence to other wants and systems, foreign to those for which they have been employed, and utter failure is the natural result. Had the various buildings been allowed to tell their own tale, to appear in their natural garb, were it rich or simple, what variety and interest would our architectural monuments present!—but no, public buildings, it was said, could not be Gothic, and therefore must be Grecian, that is, with pediments and porticos. The reasons assigned were,—1st, That Gothic was so very expensive, which is a positive falsehood; and, 2ndly, That they would not be in character. Now, how an edifice that is to consist of doors, windows, walls, roofs, and chimneys, when consistently treated, and these various features made parts of the design, can be *less in character*, than a building where they are bunglingly concealed and disguised, it is impossible to imagine. Yet this view, so utterly false and absurd, has taken such hold on the minds of the million, that

pointed architecture is considered, even at the present time, as out of the
question when public offices, law courts, bridges, and similar structures,
are in question; and the erection of the Parliament Houses in the
national style is by far the greatest advance that has yet been gained
in the right direction.[6] Although it is impossible to notice in the limits
of this tract a hundredth part of the monstrous inconsistencies which are
to be found in every modern erection; yet, to illustrate the truth of the
position I have advanced, it will be necessary to notice some of the
edifices that have been recently executed.

The Railways, had they been naturally treated, afforded a fine scope
for grand massive architecture. Little more was required than buttresses,
weathering, and segmental arches, resistance to *lateral* and *perpendicular
pressure*.[7] I do not hesitate to say, that, by merely following out the
work that was required to its natural conclusion, building exactly what
was wanted in the simplest and most substantial manner,—mere construction, as the old men weathered the flanking walls of their defences,
—tens of thousands of pounds could have been saved on every line,
and grand and durable masses of building been produced; but from

---

[6] The long lines of fronts and excessive repetition are certainly not in accordance with
the ancient spirit of civil architecture, but the detail is most consoling. We have the
arms and badges of a long succession of our kings; images of ecclesiastical, military, and
royal personages; appropriate legends in beautiful text run on every scroll: each emblem
is characteristic of our country. The internal decoration is to be of a purely national
character,—the absurdities of mythology utterly rejected,—and, if the architect's design
for the great tower be carried out, we shall have a monument of English art which has
not been surpassed even in antiquity. This building is the morning star of the great
revival of national architecture and art: it is a complete and practical refutation of those
men who venture to assert that pointed architecture is not suitable for public edifices; for
the plan embodies every possible convenience of access, light, and distribution of the various
halls and chambers, without the aid of false doors, blank windows, mock pediments, adapted
temple fronts, and show domes, to make up an elevation.

[7] See Plate III.

PL.III.

THE GRAND CAB AND OMNIBUS ENTRANCE.

A SHOW FRONT WITH CONVENIENT ADDITIONS &

RAILWAY BRIDGES ON THE ANTIENT PRINCIPLES

inconsistency, whenever any thing sublime has been attempted at the stations, the result is perfectly ridiculous.

In every instance the architects have evidently considered it an opportunity for *showing off what they could do*, instead of *carrying out what was required*. Hence the colossal Grecian portico or gateway, 100 feet high, for the cabs to drive through, and set down a few feet further, at the 14-inch brick wall and sash-window booking-office.[8] This piece of Brobdignaggian absurdity must have cost the company a sum which would have built a first-rate station, replete with convenience, and which would have been really grand from its simplicity. The Great Western stations, where any architectural display has been attempted, are mere caricatures of pointed design,—mock castellated work, huge tracery, shields without bearings, ugly mouldings, no-meaning projections, and all sorts of unaccountable breaks, to make up a design at once costly, and offensive, and full of pretension. Then the reasons which have instigated the various styles are so very absurd. At Rugby, because Rugby School, as rebuilt lately, has bad battlements and turrets, the old station had four half-turrets with the best side turned out, and a few sham loop-holes; a little further on, Gothic is dispensed with, and the barrack style prevails; at either end, two modern Greek buildings of colossal dimensions, both of which are utterly useless. The London gateway could not shelter a porter; while the Birmingham entrance was so unsuitable for its purpose, that the company have been obliged to erect various sheds right up to the large columns, and tack on a brick house, to make it at all available for its intended purpose.

These two gigantic piles of unmeaning masonry, raised at an enormous cost, are a striking proof of the utter disregard paid by architects to the *purposes* of the building, they are called upon to design; and many thousands have been fairly thrown away on every line in the erection of show fronts, and inconsistent and useless decoration.

[8] See Plate III.

The new Cemetery Companies have perpetrated the grossest absurdities in the buildings they have erected. Of course there are a superabundance of inverted torches, cinerary urns, and pagan emblems, tastefully disposed by the side of neat gravel walks, among cypress trees and weeping willows.

The central chapel is generally built on such a comprehensive plan as to be adapted (in the modern sense) for each sect and denomination in turn, as they may require its temporary use; but the entrance gateway is usually selected for the grand display of the company's enterprise and taste, as being well calculated from its position to induce persons to patronize the undertaking by the purchase of shares or graves. This is generally Egyptian, probably from some associations between the word catacombs, which occurs in the prospectus of the company, and the discoveries of Belzoni on the banks of the Nile; and nearly opposite the Green Man and Dog public-house, in the centre of a dead wall (which serves as a cheap medium of advertisement for blacking and shaving-strop manufacturers), a cement caricature of the entrance to an Egyptian temple, $2\frac{1}{2}$ inches to the foot, is erected, with convenient lodges for the policeman and his wife, and a neat pair of cast iron hieroglyphical gates, which would puzzle the most learned to decipher; while, to prevent any mistake, some such words as " New Economical Compressed Grave Cemetery Company " are inscribed in *Grecian* capitals along the frieze, interspersed with hawk-headed divinities, and surmounted by a huge representation of the winged Osiris bearing a gas lamp.[9]

The new building of St. Paul's School is another flagrant instance of the inconsistency of modern design. No sooner had the architect received the commission of erecting a building for this ancient foundation, than he turned to his stale collection of pagan authors for the authorities and details of an edifice, that was instituted by one of the

---

[9] See Plate IV.

ENTRANCE GATEWAY FOR A NEW CEMETERY

most pious churchmen of England for the education of Christian youths; and nothing better suggested itself to his narrow mind, than an unmeaning portico raised on stilts, serving only to darken the apartments over which it projects, an incipient dome, and a pagan frieze; and this wretched jumble of incongruities has cost twice the amount, and I speak advisedly, for which a truly appropriate structure, in accordance with the founder's intentions, could have been erected. It is probable that the architect never turned to study the life and intentions of Dean Colet, the learned and worthy ecclesiastic to whose pious munificence the school owes its existence, or he might have been moved to give some natural expression to the building which was intended to fulfil so pious a design. The intentions of the Dean were most edifying; the ancient edifice was dedicated in honour of the Child Jesus; the founder was evidently desirous of placing before the youthful inmates our Redeemer as an obedient Child, knowing all things, Lord of all, yet subject to his earthly parents. What could have been better calculated to have infused the principles of a holy life into the minds of the scholars? What edifying sculptures of the various incidents of our Redeemer's infancy might have ornamented the front of this building! Within the ancient school-room was an image of our Lord in the temple, teaching the doctors, before which the poor scholars sung a daily hymn and litany: but of all this not a vestige remains; and in lieu of holy Name or deed, we have fifty bulls' heads decorated for pagan sacrifice, *copied from the temple of the Sibyls*, with not so much as an image of the pious founder in a niche, to awaken the remembrance of departed worth in the hearts and minds of those, who daily benefit by Colet's bounty.

The new buildings of Christ's Hospital, although they certainly are free from the absurdities of paganism, are utterly deficient in the spirit of ancient design and arrangement. The opening towards Newgate Street might be mistaken for the back way to the Compter, or a place where relatives might hold intercourse with the inmates of that prison.

Although the tops of the posts which hold the gas lamps are ornamented with some canopy work, they look exceedingly modern, and are another striking proof of the inutility of employing the decoration without the spirit of the old men.   The hospital being destined for a place of study and education, it should have been bounded towards the street with a lofty and massive enclosure wall, entered through a regular tower gate-house, like those in the Universities, with an image of the founder in a niche, the arms of the city and of the hospital in the spandrils, and appropriate legends and inscriptions.

One fine cloistered quadrangle of the original monastery was standing; another could have been added, with the refectory and necessary buildings, in the same severe style.   The new dining-hall is designed on the very opposite principles to those which influenced the ancient builders.   The walls of the old refectories *were comparatively low*, with a *high pitch of roof*: here, the walls are enormously high, with lofty windows, like a chapel, and covered by a flat roof; and, to make the case still worse, the roof of the building is not the ceiling of the hall, but this is a mere lath-and-plaster imitation, several feet below the actual covering.

This edifice is, moreover, only *Gothic on one side*; for, if by chance the spectator turns the corner, he perceives an elevation not at all dissimilar to that of the Fleet Prison towards Farringdon Street.[10]   As for

---

[10] This wretched principle of making *pointed masks* for buildings pervades nearly all the designs of what are termed the leading architects of the day. They work only for show and effect, and neglect every portion of the building that does not meet the public eye.   On going over Lambeth Palace, I was particularly struck, on opening a door from the new buildings (which are intended to be pointed, and externally have much good detail), to find myself in a kitchen court that might have been in the rear of the Euston Hotel. The architect had evidently laid aside his Gothic *domino*, and appeared in the regular sash-window style, while under the lee of his principal elevation; taking care, however, to resume his disguise as soon as he shot out into public observation. Now, although it would be most absurd and inconsistent to employ the same detail and enrichments on all sides of a building placed in an enclosed position, yet the spirit of construction should

the new dormitories and the buildings erected on the site of the old grammar school, they are strange piles of *debased* design; but in this respect the architect may have been influenced with reference to the period when the school was founded.

Altogether, the works of Christ's Hospital are sad failures, owing to their not being conceived in the ancient spirit; but still it must be owned, in justice, that when they were commenced, so little were the real principles of Christian architecture understood or recognised,[11] that

---

remain unchanged, even in the meanest offices. By simple chamfers and weatherings, the mere essentials of good masonry, the character is perfectly maintained in every portion of the old buildings; and, what is most important, *naturally maintained;* that is, it would be impossible to do them better in any other way. *Details of this kind* do not require *designing,* but only *constructing.* For instance, the best gate must be the *strongest framed;* the sharp edges must be taken off the stiles and rails without weakening the joints and shoulders; they are chamfered and stinted, and the gate must and will look admirably well, and, of course, be in character with a pointed building, because a pointed building is a *natural building. In matters of ordinary use, a man must go out of his way to make a bad thing:* hence, in some of the rural districts, where workmen had not been poisoned by modern ideas; barns, sheds, &c., were built and framed, till very lately, on the true old principles, with braces, knees, and the high pitch. So little, however, have most modern architects any idea of beautiful effects that are produced by natural combinations and construction, that in most pointed buildings they design the mere fronts, and give up all these minor details in despair, as being so *expensive to carry out;* when, in fact, *treated consistently,* they *cost less* than the *ordinary sort of fittings, and are twice as durable.* This point is so important, that I trust, before long, to produce a treatise on *Natural Architecture,* where all these matters will be considered in detail.

[11] The progress which the revival of pointed architecture has made within the last few years is most surprising; and, if it goes on in the same ratio, there is no doubt that many architects of the day will hardly bear to look upon their present works in the course of a few years. In my own case I can truly state, that in buildings which I erected but a short time since, I can perceive numerous defects and errors, which I should not now commit; and, but a few years ago, I perpetrated abominations. Indeed, till I discovered those laws of pointed design, which I set forth in my 'True Principles,' I had no fixed rules to work upon, and frequently fell into error and extravagance. I designed and drew from a sort of intuitive feeling for Christian architecture, in conse-

it would have been difficult to have found any one, who could have done much better than the architect employed. It is a positive duty to point out all these defects, to prevent others from falling into similar errors; but, at the same time, we cannot but feel a personal respect for a man, who endeavoured to revive the old thing, at a time when there were few to sympathise or encourage.

The street elevations of the Bank of England are certainly the most costly masses of absurdities that have ever been erected. It appears to have been the aim of the architect to perpetrate as many unreal features as possible in a wall. Sometimes we have a row of *blank windows;* sometimes a *blocked-up entrance,* five feet from the ground;—now the wall is set back to diminish the internal space, and a row of columns occupies its place, well railed up to prevent any body getting under the recess;—now it rises up, to make a break, and support some stone urns and amphoræ, to hide the chimney stacks and skylights. But the grand feature is the N. W. angle, terminated by a portico, which, in addition to having *its doorway blocked up from the beginning, has its pavement several feet above the street,* without steps or means of access, *actually laid with spikes (!!!)* thickly interspersed with fragments of decaying orange-peel, stones, sticks, and bats, thrown there by the little boys, who used occasionally to climb up and get behind the columns before the introduction of the chevaux-de-frise.

It is impossible to state the vast sums that have been expended on the various absurdities of this inconsistent building; but, at a moderate

---

quence of the numerous examples I had seen. I entered into all the beauties of the style, *but I did not apply them with the feelings and on the principles of the old architects.* I was *only an adapter,* and often guilty of gross inconsistency. But, from the moment I understood that the beauty of architectural design depended on its being the expression of what the building required, and that for Christians that expression could only be correctly given by the medium of pointed architecture, all difficulties vanished; and I feel quite satisfied that when this principle becomes generally understood, good, consistent, and picturesque masses of building will arise, with all the variety and beauty of olden times.

computation, they would have erected the edifice, with all possible convenience and strength, and in a massive and appropriate character, three times over; and there then would have been, to use a commercial phrase, a good balance in hand for other purposes.

Unfortunately for themselves and the public, the Bank Directors appear to have more money than architectural judgment: hence, unmeaning features and details are crowded together, to make their buildings costly, and the Soanean eccentricities in which they have indulged so long seem only to have led them to continue the meretricious system under another management, if we may judge by the decorations of the New Dividend Office, where a room for the mere transaction of ordinary business is overloaded with all sorts of unmeaning plaster ornament, stuck up without the slightest propriety, or reference to the purpose of the building.

The Halls of the various Companies, that have been rebuilt at such an enormous cost, are really distressing to look upon. The origin and history of these companies, connected as they are with that of the City itself and many illustrious characters, afforded a fine scope for appropriate decoration, both in windows and on walls. For a hall, a noble roof of oak, with quaint device and legend, with Dais and Oriel, would seemingly have suggested itself as a matter of course to the architect, especially as many of the ancient buildings formerly belonging to these companies are actually figured in topographical works. The old kitchen, with its chimney and louvre, the buttery, and capacious cellarage in vaulted crypt beneath the hall, formed so many beautiful features of the ancient design: the rich sideboards of plate, the portraits of departed worthies, the banners and devices that hung aloft, the appropriate 'subtilties' that garnished the feast, are all described by the old chroniclers; the very barges still used by the companies might have suggested good ideas; but no,—a square mass, with a few meagre lines and breaks, Ionic caps and a flat pediment, is the extent to which the imaginations of the *great* architects of the day could reach; and at

the main entrance into the city, one of the richest companies has erected
a building vastly resembling the sort of edifices they set up for commercial banks in the larger provincial towns.

The present roof of the Guildhall itself is an abomination, and disgraceful to the civic authorities. The lower portions of the vast room
are beautiful in character; and if the ancient roof was restored with all
its appropriate devices, and enriched with colour and gilding, the Guildhall would be worthy of the city, and second only to the Regal hall
at Westminster. The expense of its restoration would be a small matter
to such a body, and the effect would surely far more than repay the
outlay.

In the New Royal Exchange we have another stale dish of ill-
adapted classicisms,—heavy, dull, and uninteresting,—nothing to awaken
national or civic associations in the minds of the citizens. Surely the
annals of one of the most ancient capitals of Europe might have suggested appropriate ideas for its Exchange, where the London worthies
of successive centuries, with their bearings and devices, might have
filled each niche. The effigies of these men, many of whom rose from
poverty and obscurity, by humble industry, to wealth and high distinction, would serve as incitements for the imitation of this and successive
generations. Every edifice, erected by such a body as the citizens of
London, should embody the dignity and character of the first commercial city in the world; it should bear the impress of its antiquity,
its honour, and privileges. Why should civic splendour be confined
to an annual water excursion, or a single procession? The banners,
the badges, the devices of the various Companies, Crafts, and Guilds,
that compose the freemen of London, are beautiful and appropriate
ornaments that should be carved on cap and wall, as well as painted
on banner and scutcheon. Those who regard these matters as childish
toys are surely mistaken in their estimate; they are honourable distinctions of skill and trade, invented by older and wiser men than
most of those who compose this generation of innovators. They form

the ties of fraternal intercourse and charity; they afford protection in decay and distress; and no one can have attentively perused the annals of London, and not admit that the various companies have been productive of immense good, and were mainly instrumental in preserving that honourable character which was formerly synonymous with an English merchant. The abuses that may at present exist among these companies, the degeneracy that is manifested in their buildings and ornaments, form no argument for their abolition. On the contrary, it should incite those in authority to revive the original practices and dignity of their various societies, and to invest their buildings, by appropriate decorations and symbols, with that local character and interest which was the distinguishing feature of the ancient buildings of London.

The absence of every thing in the architecture of the New Exchange calculated to awaken these local associations is truly lamentable. We see nothing but huge pilasters, cornices, columns, and pediments,—the same things that have been done one hundred times over, larger or smaller, in front of hotels, preaching-houses, news-rooms, and museums. It was a fine opportunity to have restored the arched ambulatory, buttressed quadrangle, high-crested roofs, and turrets of old English architecture, with a lofty clocher or bell tower, of grand proportions, like those which yet remain in the Flemish towns, and were formerly to be found in all our cities. This might have contained a fine peal to herald in the civic solemnities, with chimes for the successive hours of the day,—large clock faces, visible from all the cardinal points, and surmounted with a grove of gilded vanes, overtopped by the famous grasshopper of Gresham. Such a building, carried out with arms, badges, images, and appropriate detail, would have been at once an ornament and illustration of the city in which it was erected, admirably adapted for the convenience of business, and certainly not more, if so costly as the present unmeaning pile.

The faults of this, in common with modern structures in general, are not so much owing to individuals as to a system. How is it possible for any good results to be achieved with the present principles of architectural education? Can we ever hope to see a Christian architect come forth from the Royal Academy itself, where deadly errors are instilled into the mind of the student, with the very rudiments of instruction? Pagan lectures, pagan designs, pagan casts and models, pagan medals, and, as a reward for proficiency in these matters, a pagan journey! When the mind of a youth is well infused with contempt for every association connected with his religion and country, he is sent forth to measure temples, and, in due time, he returns to form the nucleus of a fresh set of small Doric men, and to infest the country with classical adaptations in Roman cement.

Of a truth, if architectural offices were stopped up, and fused as they serve wasps' nests in the country, we should be freed from a mass of poisonous matter that is still depositing in these places. God grant me the means, and I would soon place architectural studies on such a footing that the glory of these latter days should be even greater than that of the former.

I would also have travelling students, but I would circumscribe their limits. Durham the destination of some,—Lincolnshire's steepled fens for others,—Northampton spires and Yorkshire's venerable piles, Suffolk and Norfolk's coasts, Oxford, Devonshire, and Warwick, each county should be indeed a school,—for each *is* a school,—where those who run may read, and where volumes of ancient art lie open for all inquirers.[12]

Then would they learn that the same perfection of design is to be found in the simplicity of the village steeple, as in the towering central spire,—in the rubble walls of a sea-coast chancel, as in the hewn ashlar and fair mouldings of the large churches,—that consistency of architectural proportion has stunted the pillars of the simple nave, and

---

[12] When the architectural student was well grounded in the traditions of his national architecture, he should then proceed to study the grand continental cathedrals and churches, especially the flower and queen of Christian Churches, the Minster at Cologne.

roofed it with massive beams, while it has lifted the shafts of the cathedral to a prodigious height, and vaulted the vast space with stone, —that architectural skill consists in embodying and expressing the structure required, and not in disguising it by borrowed features. The peasant's hut, the yeoman's cottage, the farmer's house, the baronial hall, may be each perfect in its kind: the student should visit village and town, hamlet and city; he should be a minute observer of the animal and vegetable creation, of the grand effects of nature. The rocky coast, the fertile valley, the extended plain, the wooded hills, the river's bank, are all grand points to work upon; and so well did the ancient builders adapt their edifices to localities, that they seemed as if they formed a portion of nature itself, grappling and growing from the sites in which they are placed.

The rubble stones and flinty beach furnish stores as rich for the natural architect, as the limestone quarry or granite rock. What beautiful diversity does the face of this dear island present,—what a school for study and contemplation,—where are to be found twenty-four cathedrals, the finest monastic buildings, thousands of parochial churches, and interesting remains of antiquity without number, all within a boundary of a few hundred miles!

The student of Christian architecture should also imbue his mind with the mysteries of his Faith, the history of the Church, the lives of those glorious Saints and Martyrs that it has produced in all ages, especially those who, by birth or mission, are connected with the remains of ancient piety in this land. He should also be well acquainted with the annals of his country,—its constitutions, laws, privileges, and dignities,—the liturgy and rubrics of the Church,—customs and ceremonies, —topographical antiquities, local peculiarities, and natural resources. The face of the country would be then no longer disfigured by incongruous and eccentric erections, compounds of all styles and countries; but we should have structures whose arrangement and detail would be in accordance with our Faith, customs, and natural traditions. Climate would again regulate forms of covering, and positions of buildings. Local interest would be restored, and English architecture assume a distinct and dignified position in the history of art; *for we do not wish to produce mere servile imitators of former excellence of any kind, but men imbued with the consistent spirit of the ancient architects, who would work on their principles, and carry them out as the old men would have done, had they been placed in similar circumstances, and with similar wants to ourselves.*

The great objection raised against the revival of our ancient architecture by the advocates of paganism is the great difference between the present habits and necessities, and those which existed at the period when pointed architecture was most flourishing. But, in reply to this difficulty, to which I have previously alluded, it will not be difficult to prove, that while we have nothing in common with Pompeian villas and Greek temples, the ancient churches and mansions furnish us with perfect types for our present purposes; and, in order to illustrate this most important subject, I have set forth in detail the intimate connexion that can be traced between the existing system and English antiquity.

Ecclesiastical Architecture.

With that portion of the English clergy who have the happiness of being in communion with the Holy See, there cannot arise any doubt whatever. They hold precisely the same faith, and in essentials retain the same ritual, as the ancient English Church. They, consequently, require precisely the same arrangement of church, the same symbols and ornaments, as were general in this country previous to the schism. The various religious communities are bound by the same rule to recite the same office, and have the same duties to perform as those who erected and used the many solemn buildings,—now, alas! in ruins,—which are scattered all over the land. These, at least, cannot plead novelties for their paganism; and in the English Catholic body, any departure from Catholic architecture is utterly inexcusable. It can only be accounted for from extreme ignorance, or extreme perverseness, both reasons equally disgraceful. The plea of poverty cannot be admitted; for it is well known that churches which are erected on Catholic traditions are less costly than pagan rooms: and in Ireland, where the externals of religion are positively shocking and painful to behold,[13] immense sums, subscribed by the zeal of the people, have been squandered

---

[13] There is no country in Europe where the externals of religion present so distressing an aspect as Ireland:—in the rural districts, the extreme of poverty, dirt, and neglect; while, in the large towns, a lavish display of the vilest trash about the altars, and burlesques of classic or pointed design for churches, most costly and most offensive. A bad copy of that wretched compound of pagan and protestant architecture, St. Pancras New Church, in London, has been erected at Ardagh, and dignified by the name of a Cathedral. The Irish journals are lavish in their praise of this and similar structures, and boast of them as honourable examples of national skill, as if there was any thing *national* in these importations of English and continental abortions. If the clergy and gentry of Ireland possessed one spark of real national feeling, they would revive and restore those solemn piles of buildings which formerly covered that island of saints, and which are associated with the holiest and most honourable recollections of her history. Many of these were indeed rude and simple; but, massive and solemn, they harmonized most perfectly with the wild and rocky localities in which they were erected. The real Irish ecclesiastical architecture might be revived at a considerably less cost than is now actually expended on the construction of monstrosities; and the ignorance and apathy of the clergy on this most important subject is truly deplorable. They seem wedded to bad, paltry, and modern ideas; and this, too, with a people who are, perhaps, of all Catholic nations existing, the most worthy of solemn churches, and who would enter fully into the spirit and use of the ancient buildings, if they had them,—men whose faith no temporal loss or suffering could subdue,— who rise before daybreak and traverse miles of country to assist at the divine Office, and who would hail with enthusiasm any return to the solemn rites of their forefathers. If religion in Ireland were only to resume its ancient solemnity in externals, it would be indeed a spectacle for angels; but, at present, such are the absurdities, indecencies, and vulgarities displayed in all matters connected with Divine worship, that, notwithstanding the edifying piety of the people, and the exemplary conduct of many of the clergy, it is impossible to assist at the celebration of religious rites without feeling acutely pained and distressed.

on architectural absurdities. Hitherto the revival of Catholic art has been rather the result of amazing zeal amongst a few noble and devout individuals, than the spontaneous act of the body; and so-called Catholic periodicals must cease to talk of splendid Grecian altars, and solemn consecrations, where some fiddler and his pupil delighted the audience with their strains, before they can occupy their proper and dignified position as the restorers of Catholic architecture and solemnity. It is most consoling, on the one hand, to know that good ideas are spreading; but humiliating to think that there should be room for the spread of ideas and opinions which should fill the heart of every British Catholic, and animate them as one man in the glorious and holy cause. And, alas! whilst a few great spirits devote their fortune and energies for the revival of departed solemnity, others of equal temporal means are content to look on with apathy, if not actually to oppose their labours. Some apparently reject tradition and authority, espouse the cause of paganism, and follow in the wake of protestant monstrosities, with the externals of a temple, and the interior of a conventicle; while the multitude neither know nor care any thing about the matter. Men of devout minds are scandalized with the foreign trumpery that is introduced on the most solemn occasions, and the noisy theatrical effects that are substituted for the solemn chants and hymns of the Church. These things are most distressing on the continent, although they are modified by the vastness of the churches and the remains of antiquity; but here, in England, where they are performed in buildings not dissimilar to assembly-rooms, they are intolerable, and must convey to the casual and uninstructed spectator the lowest idea of Catholic rites. It is painful to see these wretched practices puffed off in Catholic journals, and described much in the same strain as is used in the Theatrical Observer, —a list of performers,—criticisms on the execution of solos and quartets during that Holy Sacrifice which fills even the angels with awe and reverence. Since Christ himself hung abandoned and bleeding on the Cross of Calvary, never has so sad a spectacle been exhibited to the afflicted Christian as is presented in many modern Catholic chapels, where the adorable Victim is offered up by the Priests of God's Church, disguised in miserable dresses intended for the sacred vestments, surrounded by a scoffing auditory of protestant sight-seekers who have paid a few shillings a head to grin at mysteries which they do not understand, and to hear the performances of an infidel troop of mercenary musicians, hired to sing symbols of faith they disbelieve, and salutations to that Holy Sacrament they mock and deny.

With respect to the present Anglican Church the case is, of course, by no means so clear and positive. Still, if she acted on her present acknowledged doctrines and discipline, without even taking into consideration any probable change in her position, she must turn to Catholic antiquity for the types of her architecture and ornament.

This argument is based on *principles and formularies;* for abuses cannot be either advanced or received in support of any position. I am not taking into account the various grades of opinion and practice that are unhappily to be found among those who act in the capacity of Anglican clergymen. I deal only with canons and rubrics; and if these were properly and universally carried out, a vast move would be made in the right direction.

1. The ancient form and arrangement of the parochial churches, consisting of nave and chancel, should be preserved. The words respecting the latter are as follow: "The chancels shall remain as in *times past;*"—and although it is a notorious fact that they did not so remain, yet their desecration was chiefly owing to the mass of illiterate functionaries, who, on the deprivation of the Catholic ecclesiastics under Elizabeth, were intruded not only into parochial cures, but into the chairs of the ancient bishoprics. In truth, the so-called reformers of the reign of Edward the Sixth and Elizabeth, and even the compilers of the Common Prayer itself, were far more protestant than the formularies which were retained, and to which they subscribed rather with the hope of being thereby able to effect further mischief and ad-

vance puritanism, than to restore departed solemnity.[14]   Under the
Primate Laud, a surprising re-action took place, unfortunate and un-
satisfactory in result, but an evident proof of the Catholic feeling which
would have developed itself in the Anglican Church, had it not been
for the pressure of the puritan faction.   But to return, taking the words
as they stand,—*The chancels shall remain as in times past;*—can there
be any reasonable doubt as to the propriety of adhering strictly to the
ancient models, of which so many truly beautiful examples remain for
imitation?

2. A tower for bells is required; and this important feature of a
church was never omitted in England even during the most debased
period of ecclesiastical architecture.   A tower naturally suggests a spire
as its termination; and where is it possible to obtain a consistent type
for church steeples, excepting from those glorious churches whose entire
architecture and arrangements were generated by the peculiar wants of
Christian rites?   This must be evident to all on inspecting the wretched
attempts at classic steeples, where pediments and porticos, pillars and
cornices, are piled upon each other like children's card houses, to make
up an elevation without any grand connecting lines or consistent arrangement,—mere forced, unnatural combinations, most offensive to the
eye, as evident endeavours to make a *vertical effect* out of the features
of *horizontal architecture.*   The rage for these pedimented and telescopic
steeples is nearly over; and the ancient spire-crowned towers, adapted
to any scale, or degree of decoration, must be universally restored.

3. Galleries are contrary to the intentions of the Anglican Church.
They are of comparatively modern origin, erected for the most part
since the Revolution; and their introduction can only be accounted for
by a similar degeneracy of spirit to that which has tolerated them in
so many modern Catholic churches, where they are far more objectionable and inconsistent.

---

[14] See the Letters of the intruded Bishops to Foreign Protestants, in Strype's Annals.

A most laudable opposition has, however, been awakened both against the erection of galleries and the modern abomination of pews, which are equally intolerable; and we may fairly hope before long to see both utterly abolished. It is not, therefore, difficult to show that an ancient church nave, with its pillars, aisles, low open carved oak benches, and southern porch, is the proper model for present imitation.

4. There is no alteration whatever allowable for ancient usage in respect of the Fonts: they are required to stand in their original position, with covers, and secured by locks. These covers may be made as lofty and ornamental as circumstances will admit. Many of them were executed during the reigns of James, and Charles the First; and although, of course, debased in details, are designed in the mass on the ancient principles, with a multitude of pinnacles and lesser canopies: of these there are two fine specimens at Newcastle-on-Tyne, and another, probably by the same artist, in Durham cathedral.

5. Pulpits, if properly placed on one side of the church, are not only unobjectionable, but necessary. Numerous examples, both of wood and stone, are to be found in the ancient English churches; and the ambones of the basilicas are of primitive antiquity. Pulpits are only offensive when intruded into the centre of the church, obscuring the Altar, and turning the back of the preacher to the seat of the sacred Mysteries: they should not be too elaborate in design, nor over large in dimensions. With respect to reading pew, and clerk's desk, they are of modern introduction; a brass or wooden lectern and a litany stool are amply sufficient. These are quite in accordance with ancient practice: the Epistle, Gospel, and Lessons were originally intended to be heard by the people, for which reason they were read from the top of the rood lofts in cathedral churches, where the choir was divided off by a close screen. The deacon, sub-deacon, or lector, out of respect for the Altar, read turned sideways to the people, while all prayers were addressed towards the East.

6. In many cases the chancel screens yet remain perfect, with much

of their ancient painting, gilding, and imagery of Saints and Apostles. They were *never removed in any case by authority*, but only from private ignorance, or love of innovation; and, so far from being opposed to Anglican custom, they are mentioned as necessary in old episcopal visitations. A screen of Italian detail, but of the old form, was erected during the last century in the church of St. Peter, Cornhill, London.

In old St. Giles's Church, Bloomsbury, erected in the seventeenth century, the chancel was separated by a large screen in the figure of a beautiful gate, on which were carved three statues,—on one side, St. Paul with his sword,—on the other, St. Barnabas with his book,—and over them, St. Peter and keys, with winged cherubim. This screen, erected at the cost of Lady Dudley, was pulled down in 1640, and sold by the puritan faction.[15] The choir screen of Wadham College Chapel, Oxford, consecrated in 1613, is a very interesting existing specimen of the continuance of the old traditional separation in the seventeenth century.

7. It is very certain that the consecrated stone Altars were sacrilegiously demolished and horribly profaned by the protestant party, both in Edward the Sixth's reign, and afterwards in the second year of Elizabeth's, and that their chief aim thereby was to abolish the idea of a sacrificial oblation among the people. But it is equally certain that their revival was attempted under a better state of things in the reign of Charles the First; and surely those who grant the authorities of Edward's time the right of demolishing, cannot deny the same right of restoration to their successors at a subsequent period. There can be but little doubt that stone Altars, placed at the eastern end of the chancel, will be generally revived: these may have frontals of the canonical colours, suited to the festivals, and richly embroidered with appropriate devices; and these frontals should not by any means be covered during the time of communion, as the white linen cloth need not be much wider than the top of the altar, and should hang down

---

[15] Parton's History of St. Giles's.

at each end. The use of lighted tapers on the altar seems to be warranted by the words, that such ornaments shall be in use, as were in use in the second year of King Edward the Sixth.[16] The candlesticks, covers of the holy gospels, chalices, &c., should be made of precisely the same form and decoration as those anciently used.

8. The two chairs, placed on each side of the communion table, are of very modern introduction, *and most unseemly*, as having their backs to the East. There can be no reason whatever for the clergy, when sitting, not occupying the sedilia, especially in cathedral churches, where the canon for the celebration of the communion requires the officiating priest to be attended by a gospeller and epistler (Canon xxiv.).

9. No doubt whatever can exist at the present time respecting the propriety of decorating churches with sacred symbols and imagery: the lively representation of the life of our blessed Redeemer, and the works and martyrdoms of the saints, cannot fail to be productive of much edification and good.

The destruction of the ancient stained glass, resplendent with sacred imagery, was mostly perpetrated by avowed puritans; and even at the worst periods there were found some good souls, who had both heart and means to preserve many of these glorious works from destruction. There are few cathedrals in Europe to compare in this respect to that of York; and many of our parochial churches are yet rich in glass. Indeed, when we reflect that during the last century the Catholic chapter of Amiens cathedral removed much of the magnificent glass of the nave, and replaced it by white panes, to *improve the effect*, and that modern Catholic ecclesiastics in France and Belgium have not only taken out the stained glass, but the mullions and tracery also, *by way of lighting the church*, we can feel less surprise at the sad losses we have sustained in England.

---

[16] Some excellent remarks on these and other matters connected with the celebration of the Anglican liturgy are contained in two sermons preached in St. James's Church, Enfield. London, 1842.

In an admirable article which recently appeared in the British Critic, the writer most justly observes, that circumstances have so changed during the last three centuries, that some of the most violent innovators, had they lived in our age of lax indifference, would have acted and written in a very different strain. This remark will apply equally respecting the use of images. There is no fear at the present time of sacred representations being regarded with superstitious reverence : there is far greater danger that, holy symbols and figures being replaced by pagan fables or bare walls, men will lose all remembrance of the glorious mysteries they represented. It must be admitted that, in opposition to true Catholic doctrine, some images were regarded by the ignorant with a superstitious veneration, and certain representations were tolerated in the churches, which were highly objectionable. There can be but little doubt that all these matters would have been reformed, without violence or occasion of scandal to weaker brethren, by the decrees of the Council of Trent; and nothing can be more absurd and unjust than persons continually raking up, at the present time, old extravagant indulgences and local practices, which have been condemned centuries ago by ecclesiastical decrees, and some hundreds of which are denounced separately in works printed by authority.

The use and intention of sacred images is to raise the heart of the spectator from the figure to the reality, and to instruct the faithful in the mysteries of religion by lively representation. The soundness of this principle is fully acknowledged by the general practice of the present time,—in the multitude of biblical illustrations prepared for the instruction of youth.

The Church only requires that honour and veneration for sacred symbols which their character naturally demands,[17] and which is essen-

---

[17] This is beautifully expressed in the following distich, inscribed over a crucifix at Antwerp :

Effigiem Christi dum transis pronus honora,
Sed non effigiem sed quem designat adora.

tially the same as that yet given in the Anglican Church to the holy Name of Jesus; and is paralleled in temporal matters by the external respect shown to the throne in the House of Peers, or the quarter-deck of a man-of-war. Sacred imagery is a noble field for the exercise of the highest powers of art; and painting and sculpture, when devoted to the service of the Church, are calculated to improve and elevate the religious feelings of a nation in a surprising degree.

Now to sum up. If, as I have shown, the Anglican Church requires bell towers, spires, naves, chancels, screens, fonts, altars, sacred symbols and ornaments, I will ask whether the types of these various features are to be found in the ancient pointed churches of England, or in the classic temples of antiquity? Surely no one can hesitate to admit at once that, in the former, we have perfect models for imitation; while, in the latter, we cannot find one corresponding arrangement or detail: and therefore, even in its present position, by its own existing canons and rubrics, the Anglican Church is bound, consistently, to work exclusively on the principles of Christian architecture, and to renounce all pagan adaptations whatsoever.

With regard to the collegiate establishments which have continued in uninterrupted succession from the time of their original foundation, and which are yet supported by the pious munificence of their founders, and profess to be governed by their ancient statutes, there cannot exist a doubt as to the propriety, if not the absolute duty, of their erecting such buildings as they may require, in the same style and spirit as those originally raised for the accommodation of their predecessors. I say *spirit* as well as *style;* for it is not merely sufficient to cut tracery and build buttresses and pinnacles, for that has been done at a vast cost and with miserable effect at King's and other colleges at Cambridge, but to preserve that scholastic gravity of character, that reverend and solemn appearance, that is found in the ancient erections. Any departure from Catholic antiquity in a college is unpardonable: the frequent daily services in the chapel, the assembly of the community in the refectory, the enclosure, the academical costume, the celibacy of the inmates, are so many relics of ancient discipline which demand a continuance of the original architecture; and in those instances where this has been neglected, not one can be pointed out which is not a miserable failure and a compound of anomalies. Are Queen's, Worcester, or the new quadrangle of Christ Church, to be compared for one instant with Merton, New College, or Magdalene? They rather resemble sick hospitals or barracks of the last century, than the abodes of piety and learning. Colonnades, pediments, and heathen gods, are but sorry substitutes for solemn cloisters, high turrets, and images of reverend founders and saintly patrons.

During the early part of the seventeenth century, under the influence of the Laudian school, some collegiate buildings were erected in a far more consistent spirit than the more recent examples. Among these, the chapel of Peter-house, at Cambridge, is remarkable: the detail is, of course, debased, but it is a very successful attempt for the period; the tracery windows are filled with stained glass; the east window, of five lights, containing the Crucifixion of our Lord, with many saints and angels in the tracery. The roof is waggon-headed, supported on corbels; the western bay forms an antechapel, being divided off by an oak screen; within this are double rows of oak stalls, with a large sanctuary.

This chapel must have been far richer in decoration when originally founded; as, in the report of the parliamentary writers in 1643, they say, "We went to Peter-house and pulled down two mighty angels "with wings, and divers other angels, with the four evangelists, and "Peter with his keys, on the chapel door, together with about one "hundred cherubim, and many superstitious letters in gold." This account will show the correct intentions which actuated the collegiate builders of even that period, and how completely paganism was excluded from their designs: it is, indeed, monstrous, now that the ancient detail is so much better understood, and the facilities of execution far greater, to see vile compounds of Italian details rising amid the glories of Catholic antiquity in both Oxford and Cambridge. It is some consolation, however, to know that neither of these edifices are intended for collegiate purposes, but as show galleries; and I question much if they will be allowed to remain even for that purpose, when the true principles of Catholic architecture are more generally disseminated among the members of the University.

Hospitals for the poor ought, undoubtedly, to be erected in a style at once simple and religious: the aged should be provided with cloisters for sheltered exercise,—a common hall and kitchen,—separate lodging chambers, and a chapel for daily devotion; religious emblems and memorials of their benefactors should constitute the only decorations, interspersed with pious scriptures and moral legends. Beautiful examples of these truly Christian institutions are to be found in the ancient hospitals of Stamford, Leicester, Northampton, and Coventry, or even in the later foundations of Whitgift at Croydon, and Abbott at Guildford.

I trust I have now set forth enough to prove that the religious edifices of England, if consistently designed, should be arranged on the same principles as the ancient buildings erected by our Catholic forefathers. They must, of course, fall far short of the glorious solemnity that can alone be attained in a truly Catholic position; but, as far as they go, they should have all in common with English antiquity, and not the slightest accordance with classic arrangement and detail.

Sepulchral Memorials.

These are so intimately connected with ecclesiastical architecture, that it seems necessary to enter upon some details on the subject before proceeding to other matters.

The principal reasons assigned by sculptors for resorting to classic costume in their monumental designs has been the unsightly form of modern habits, which would render the effigy of the deceased ludicrous in appearance, if represented with them.

This would be perfectly true if it were necessary, or even correct, to adopt the ordinary costume of domestic life in such cases; but it is scarcely possible to find any person sufficiently dignified in station to warrant an effigy, who does not hold some official situation, either ecclesiastical, civil, or military; the robes and insignia of which, if properly and severely represented, would produce effigies little inferior in solemn effect to the ancient ones.[18] To represent persons of the present century in the costume of the fourteenth, is little less inconsistent than to envelope them in the Roman toga. As I have before said, architecture and art should be a consistent expression of the period, and it will not be difficult to show, that, adhering strictly to these principles, we can in the present age revive the most solemn and Christian memorials of the dead.[19]

ECCLESIASTICAL PERSONS.

For the English clergy, there is not the slightest difficulty; those in communion with the Holy See using the same number and character of sacred vestments as of old.

Bishops.—Amice, albe, stole, tunic and dalmatic, maniple, with chasuble or cope, mitre and staff, buskins and sandals.

Priests.—Amice, albe, plain or apparelled, stole, maniple and chasuble, holding a chalice with the most Holy Sacrament.

---

[18] The ancient monumental effigies invariably represent the deceased persons in their robes of state. Kings, bishops, priests, nobles, knights and their ladies, are habited in a manner to express most fully their dignities and office, with a profusion of heraldic devices illustrative of their birth and descent.

[19] The present female costume is by no means ill-adapted for sepulchral brasses. In the annexed Plate three are engraved, which are accurately copied from those in use. The devout position of the hands contributes greatly to the solemn effect. (See Plate V.)

✠ EXAMPLES OF MODERN COSTUME ADAPTED TO SEPULCHRAL BRASSES

Deacons.—Amice, albe, and dalmatic, stole and maniple, holding the book of the Holy Gospels.

Sub-deacons.—Amice, albe, tunic and maniple, with an empty chalice.

Minor orders.
$\left\{\begin{array}{l}\text{Ostiarius}\\\text{Lector}\\\text{Exorcist}\\\text{Acolyth}\end{array}\right\}$ in surplices with $\left\{\begin{array}{l}\text{keys.}\\\text{book.}\\\text{hands joined in prayer.}\\\text{cruets and candlestick.}\end{array}\right.$

These various dignities may be expressed, without effigy, by a cross fleury, with the pastoral staff, chalice, book, or other instruments represented by the side.

The Anglican churchmen should be habited as follows:

Bishops—in cassock, rochet, with a cope; and there are instances of the pastoral staff even in the seventeenth century.

Priests—in cassock, albe (plain), with a cope or chasuble.

Deacons—in an albe.

Effigies of clergy habited in surplices, with hoods,[20] would be perfectly correct, and of these there are many ancient examples.

These habits would be rather in accordance with Anglican *rubrics* than practice; but they are enjoined by the present canons, and, though long neglected, through the combined influence of indifference and puritan principles, they will be doubtless restored with the revival of reverence and solemnity.

CIVIL PERSONAGES.

The Sovereign should be represented in the Royal robes which are still used in the coronation, and which are precisely the same in number and description as those used in the days of St. Edward. There is no reason for not substituting appropriate and better designed ornaments in lieu of those which are generally embroidered, and a more beautiful form

---

[20] The present manner of wearing hoods hanging half down the back is most absurd. They should come close up to the neck, with the ends falling from each shoulder in front, as represented in the old monumental brasses.

of crown than that actually in use:[21] a recumbent effigy, habited in these robes, with the orb and sceptre, would not be inferior in dignity and effect to those truly royal monuments in Westminster Abbey Church, and would form an admirable contrast to the miserable memorials of the English sovereigns of the last century at Windsor.

The various ranks of nobility should be represented in the state robes peculiar to their several degrees, with their various family badges and heraldic distinctions; those who were Knights of the Garter or other orders, with their mantles, collars, and other insignia,—the lion and dog, emblems of courage and fidelity, couchant at their feet. When on high tombs, the niches round the sides may be most appropriately filled by smaller effigies of relations, habited as mourners for the deceased, with their several shields of arms. These are frequently introduced round the ancient monuments, and might be revived with the greatest propriety.

Judges should, of course, be represented in their robes,—Heralds, in their tabards,—Doctors of Medicine and Music, in the habit of their degrees,—Aldermen and civic functionaries, in their gowns of office;— and for private gentlemen even, a long cloak, disposed in severe folds, would produce a solemn effect.

For the humbler classes, a cross, with the instruments of their trades or crafts, with marks and devices, would be sufficient and appropriate; and, in a rural district, a mere wooden or stone cross, with the name of the deceased.

There is not, in fact, the least practical difficulty in reviving at the present time consistent and Christian monuments for all classes of persons,[22] and at the same cost now bestowed on pagan abominations,

---

[21] The present crown is far too heavy and clumsy, and is not very dissimilar in form to a lamp top. Still it is consoling to see that it is surmounted by a cross; and the circlet is yet alternated with crosses and fleurs-de-lis, emblematic of our Divine Redeemer and Blessed Lady.

[22] The annexed Plate represents brasses and other sepulchral monuments of a Christian character, that have been lately revived. (See Plate VI.)

+ REVIVED SEPULCHRAL BRASSES +

which disfigure both the consecrated enclosure which surrounds the church, and the interior of the sacred building itself. Surely the Cross must be the most appropriate emblem on the tombs of those who profess to believe in God crucified for the redemption of man; and it is almost incredible, that while the dead are interred in consecrated ground, and in the ancient position,—prayers for their souls' repose acknowledged to be of apostolical antiquity, and the office recited at their interment composed from the ancient ritual,—the types of all modern sepulchral monuments should be essentially pagan; and urns, broken pillars, extinguished lamps, inverted torches, and sarcophagi, should have been substituted for recumbent effigies, angels, and emblems of mercy and redemption.

Civil Architecture.

It will not be difficult to show that the wants and purposes of Civil Buildings now are almost identical with those of our English forefathers. In the first place, climate, which necessarily regulates the pitch of roofs, light, warmth, and internal arrangement, remains of course precisely the same as formerly. Secondly, we are governed by nearly the same laws and same system of political economy. The Sovereign, with the officers of state connected with the crown,—the Houses of Peers and Commons,—the judges of the various courts of law, and form of trial,—the titles and rank of the nobility,—the tenures by which their lands are held, and the privileges they enjoy,—the corporate bodies and civic functionaries,—are all essentially the same as in former days.

There is no country in Europe which has preserved so much of her ancient system as England. We still see the grey tower of the parochial church rising by the side of the manorial house; and, in many instances, the chantry chapel yet remains, with a long succession of family monuments, from the armed crusader to that of the parent of the actual possessor.

The palace of the Sovereign of such a country should exhibit the evidence of dignified antiquity in every detail. Surely the long succession of our kings,—their noble achievements,—the honourable badges and charges that they bore, — would form subjects which would naturally suggest themselves for the decorations of the various halls and apartments. How truly grand and national would a building thus designed and ornamented appear, where not only the general character, but every detail, was expressive of the dignity of the country, and an illustration of its history ! And are not the examples for such an edifice to be found in the ancient glories of St. Stephen's and Windsor, the habitations of our Edwards and Henrys ?—The mere dining-hall of the former, in its present denuded state, without tapestry, glass, or enrichment, conveys a far grander impression to the mind of the beholder than the most gorgeously decorated chambers of modern times ; and what a splendid effect would be produced if one of those ancient palaces, so suited for the residence of a Christian monarch, were restored, with all its appropriate furniture and decorations !

The same remarks apply with equal force to the residences of the nobility and gentry. How painful is it to behold, in the centre of a fine old English park and vast domain, a square unsightly mass of bastard Italian, *without one expression of the faith, family, or country of the owner !* How contrary to the spirit of the ancient mansions, covered with ancestral badges and memorials, and harmonizing in beautiful irregularity with the face of nature !

Any modern invention which conduces to comfort, cleanliness, or durability, should be adopted by the consistent architect ; *to copy a thing merely because it is old, is just as absurd as the imitations of the modern pagans.* Our domestic architecture should have a peculiar expression illustrative of our manners and habits : *as the castle merged into the baronial mansion, so it may be modified to suit actual necessities ;* and the smaller detached houses which the present state of society has generated, should possess a peculiar character : they are only objectionable

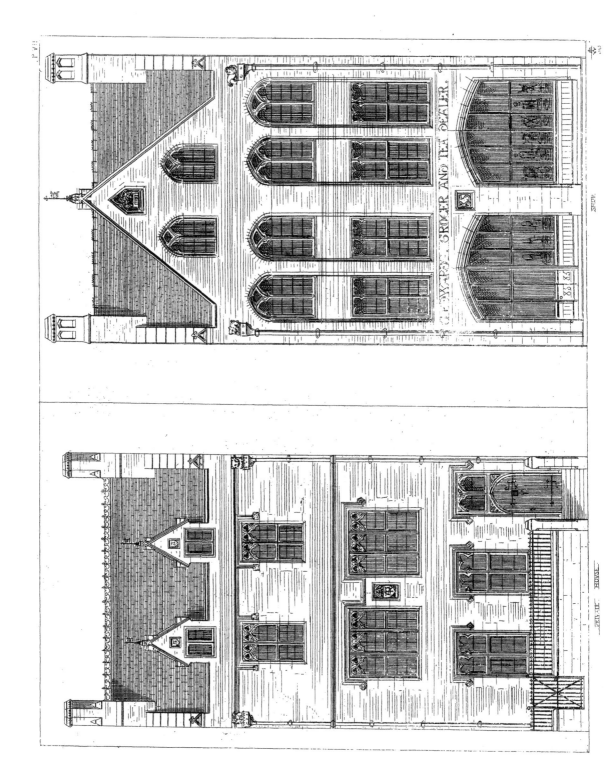

when made to appear diminutive representations of larger structures. And it is not only possible, but easy, to work on the same consistent principles as our ancestors in the erection of all our domestic buildings.

It would be absurd, with our present resources, to build wooden houses in towns, which originated with the superabundance of that material in former times, and the difficulty of transporting stone or brick; but brick fronts, adapted perfectly to internal convenience, and in accordance with the legal provisions for town buildings, may be erected, which are capable of producing excellent effect, if consistently treated, and terminated by the natural form of the gable.[23]

There is no reason in the world why noble cities, combining all possible convenience of drainage, water-courses, and conveyance of gas,[24] may not be erected in the most consistent and yet Christian character. *Every building that is treated naturally, without disguise or concealment, cannot fail to look well.*

If our present domestic buildings were only designed in accordance with their actual purposes, they would appear equally picturesque with the old ones! Each edifice would tell its own tale, and, by diversity of character, contribute to the grand effect of the whole.

Modern Inventions and Mechanical Improvements.

In matters purely mechanical, the Christian architect should gladly avail himself of those improvements and increased facilities that are suggested from time to time. The steam engine is a most valuable power for sawing, raising, and cleansing stone, timber, and other materials. The old masons used wheels of great diameter in the erection of their buildings: this was, of course, a great increase of power over mere

---

[23] See Plate VII.

[24] A gas lamp, if designed simply with reference to its use, would be an inoffensive object; but when it is composed of a Roman altar, surmounted by the fasces, and terminated by an incense tripod, it becomes perfectly ridiculous.

manual strength; and had they been acquainted with a greater, they would undoubtedly have used it. Why should ten minutes be expended in raising a body which could be equally well done in two? The readier and cheaper the *mechanical* part of building can be rendered, the greater will be the effect for the funds; and if I were engaged in the erection of a vast church, I should certainly set up an engine that would saw blocks, turn detached shafts, and raise the various materials to the required heights. By saving and expedition in these matters, there would be more funds and a greater amount of manual labour to expend on enrichments and variety of detail.

The whole history of Pointed Architecture is a series of inventions: time was when the most beautiful productions of antiquity were novelties. *It is only when mechanical invention intrudes on the confines of art, and tends to subvert the principles which it should advance, that it becomes objectionable.* Putty pressing, plaster and iron casting for ornaments, wood burning, &c., are not to be rejected because such methods were unknown to our ancestors, *but on account of their being opposed in their very nature to the true principles of art and design,*—by substituting monotonous repetitions for beautiful variety, flatness of execution for bold relief, encouraging cheap and false magnificence, and reducing the varied principles of ornamental design, which should be in strict accordance with the various buildings and purposes in which it is used, to a mere ready-made manufacture. But while, on the one hand, we should utterly reject the use of castings as substitutes for ornamental sculpture, we should eagerly avail ourselves of the great improvements in the working of metals for constructive purposes.

Had the old builders possessed our means of obtaining and working iron, they would have availed themselves of it to a great extent. The want of proper ties has occasioned most serious settlements, and even the destruction of some of the finest Christian edifices,—the very weight and massiveness of the work causing it frequently to settle and give. And there is scarcely a tower of great dimensions erected during the middle ages, which it has not been necessary to tie together by iron chains and key wedges at a subsequent period. Now, it must be evident that if these ties were built in the first instance in the body of the work, they would be free from the action of atmosphere, and prevent both fissures and the spreading of the work which would render their ultimate employment necessary.

In a cruciform church these precautions are most necessary. The lateral thrust of nave, transept, and choir arches, both of aisles and triforium, rest against the four great central pillars, which are only enabled to resist the pressure by the weight of the great tower resting on them. But this in many cases was insufficient, and, when they began to give, has hastened their destruction. Hence the inverted arches at Wells, and the screens at Salisbury and Canterbury, which have been added long subsequently to the erection of the original buildings, to confine the pillars from giving inwards. At Amiens they are tied by immense chains extending the whole length of the nave and choir.

Had this point been considered in the original structures, the pressure might have been effectually counteracted, by inserting iron shafts in the centre of the great piers, and chains from them in the thickness of the triforium and clerestory, reaching to the four extremities of the building. I merely mention this one fact, amongst a number that might be adduced, to show that we possess facilities and materials unknown to our ancestors, and which would have greatly added to the stability of the structures they erected. *We do not want to arrest the course of inventions, but to confine these inventions to their legitimate uses,* and *to prevent their substitution for nobler arts.*

We approve highly of cast iron for constructive purposes, while we denounce it as the meagre substitute for masons' skill. We would gladly employ Roman cement in brick walling, while we abominate it in the mock erections of the day. We consider branding irons exceedingly useful for marking owners' and makers' names on carts and implements of trade, but we cannot allow them to replace the carver's art.

In a word, we should neither cling pertinaciously to ancient methods of building, solely on the score of antiquity, nor reject inventions because of their novelty, but try both by sound and consistent principles, and act accordingly.

Another great mistake of modern times is the supposition that Christian architecture will not afford sufficient scope for the art of sculpture. So far from this, while a Greek temple admits only of such decoration in the pediment and round the frieze, every portion of a Christian church may and should be covered with sculpture of the most varied kind,—vegetable, animal, and the human figure, in wonderful diversity of position and aspect; sometimes single in niches, sometimes in groups of high relief, and in subjects of the most majestic character. At the entrances of the church, the lessening arches, which form the vast recesses, are lined with angels, patriarchs, prophets, kings, martyrs, bishops, and confessors;[25] above the doorways, the genealogy of our Divine Redeemer, his birth, passion, the doom or final judgment,—subjects which, it must be admitted, afford the fullest scope for the developement of the highest powers of human skill. While the whole exterior of the sacred edifice, even to the summit of the towers, may be covered with images and sculpture, the interior presents an equally extensive field for the exercise of art in all possible variety of size and position, from the minute groups of the stall seats, to the long line of sacred history that surrounds the choir; from the enrichments of the aisle walls, level with the eye, to the sculptured bosses, luxuriant in foliage and rich in imagery, that key the vaulted roof at an immense elevation. Flaxman[26] was the first of

---

[25] Casts from some of these images at Notre Dame, Paris, which have lately been brought over to the School of Design, are wonderful examples of Christian art.

[26] Had Flaxman lived a few years later, he would have been a great Christian artist; but in his day men never thought it possible to do any thing fine in art that was not derived from paganism: hence his great powers were unhappily expended in illustrating fables of classic antiquity, instead of embodying edifying truths. His observations on the excellence of our Catholic ancestors, and his lamentations on the destruction of their works, are heartfelt

FROM THE SOVTH PORCH OF ROVEN CATHEDRAL Cᵗʸ

OVER NW DOORWAY Rᴴ CATHˡ C 1260

CEMETERY NVREMBERG 15 CENᵗ

IN IVORY 14ᵗ CENᵗ

✠ EXAMPLES OF THE CHRISTIAN SCHOOL OF SCVLPTVRE

the modern school who bore testimony both to the excellence of Christian sculpture and the scope that was afforded for the exercise of the art in pointed structures. His lectures contain several remarks on the admirable works executed in the English cathedrals, even while art was at a comparatively low ebb in Italy. There is in fact no difference of *principle* between the fine draperied works of the classic sculptors and those of the middle ages; the difference is in the *objects represented* and the motives of the artists. The principal object of the former was to display the human figure, which the latter, from the Christian principle of modesty, rather concealed. *The pagans wished to perpetuate human feelings,—the Christians, the divine.*[27]

But to talk of Gothic and Grecian drapery in sculpture as distinct in principle, is absurd; the art of either period *is a grand expression of nature*, and the distinct character is produced by the change of habits in the middle ages for those of classic antiquity. We have the cope instead of a toga, and the chasuble for a tunic. There is also a great difference in the texture of the various stuffs, the square folds of the Christian images being produced by the material then in use. Different circumstances and systems must generate different expressions of art. Phidias himself, had he worked under the influence of the Christian faith, would have exhibited equal skill in abstract art, but with a very different developement.

The great error of modern sculptors is their servile imitation of classic art, without endeavouring to embody existing principles in their works. Unless art is the expression of the system it should illustrate, it loses

---

and eloquent; and when we consider that at the period he wrote, the most glorious works of the middle ages were treated with apathy and even derision, the Christian artist of the present time must feel grateful for the good he effected by setting forth neglected truth. We can only regret that he did not follow out his convictions to their legitimate results, at least in the sepulchral monuments that were intrusted to him, for he does not appear to have executed one which had the slightest reference to Catholic traditions.

[27] See Plate VIII.

at once its greatest claim on admiration, and fails to awaken any feelings of sympathy in the heart of the spectator.

Since the fifteenth century, the saints of the Church have been made to resemble, as closely as possible, heathen divinities. *The Christian mysteries have been used as a mere vehicle for the revival of pagan forms and the exhibition of the artist's anatomical skill.* They were no longer productions to edify the faithful, but to advance the fame of the author; and all consistency and propriety was sacrificed for this unworthy end.[28]

The albe of purity and chaste girdle were exchanged for light and often indecent costume, to exhibit the human figure after the manner of an opera dancer; and modern artists were so imbued with classic design and ideas, that when they attempted to work for the Church, their representations of the mysteries of religion were scarcely recognisable from the fables of mythology.[29] We do not want to revive a facsimile of the works or style of any particular individual, or even period; *but it is the devotion, majesty, and repose of Christian art, for which we are contending;*—it is not a *style*, but a *principle.* Surely all the improvements that are consequent on the study of anatomy and the proportions of the human figure can be engrafted on ancient excellence; and an image, in correct costume, and treated in accordance with Catholic traditions, would afford equal scope for the display of the sculptor's art as a half-naked figure in a distorted attitude, more resembling a maniac who had hastily snatched a blanket for a covering than a canonized saint.

Did our artists of the present time work with the same faith and humility as the old men, and strive *to express the doctrines of the Church rather than their own peculiar notions,* we might soon have a school

---

[28] See Plate IX.

[29] It is but just to remark, that the modern German school, with the great Overbeck, are not only free from this reproach, but deserving of the warmest eulogiums and respect for their glorious revival of Christian art and traditions.

Pl IX

GROUP FROM THE ASSUMPTION
BY CORREGIO AT PARMA 16 CENT.

VATICAN LIBRARY TIME OF SIXTUS V

ITALIAN 16 CENT

ANGELS FROM ST PETERS ROME 12 CENT

ANGELS BY GIOTTO

ITALIAN OF THE 14 CENT

GERMAN ABOUT 1500

CONCEPTIONS OF ANGELIC SPIRITS BY OLD CHRISTIAN
AND REVIVED PAGAN ARTISTS

of sculpture equal in sentiment and devotion, and superior in anatomical correctness, to that which existed during the ages of faith.

In conclusion, it must appear evident that the present revival of ancient architecture in this country is based on the soundest and most consistent principles. It is warranted by religion, government, climate, and the wants of society. It is a perfect expression of all we should hold sacred, honourable, and national, and connected with the holiest and dearest associations; nor is there in the whole world a country which is better calculated for the revival of ancient excellence and solemnity than England. We have immense power, vast wealth, and great though often misdirected zeal. Sounder views and opinions are daily gaining ground,—feelings of reverence for the past increasing in an extraordinary degree; and, with all her faults, we must remember that England, while she was the last to abandon Christian architecture, has been foremost in hailing and aiding its revival. Even in the worst and darkest times of pagan and protestant ascendancy, some of her sons were found able and willing advocates of her ancient glory; and, notwithstanding the repeated mutilations they have undergone, and the sad destruction of the monastic churches, our ecclesiastical edifices exhibit far more perfect traces of their ancient beauty than is to be found in many continental buildings, which, although they have escaped the hammer of the fanatic, have been more fatally injured from the chisels and pencils of revived pagan artists.

We should not try the deeds of England during the last three centuries by those which preceded them, *but by the corresponding history of surrounding nations;* and we shall find that throughout the Christian world, the period which has intervened since the sixteenth century has been one of bitter trial and degradation to the Church. Wherever we go, we see the great ecclesiastical works arrested at the same period,—towers half erected, naves unfinished, details uncarved,—either a total stoppage of works, or bastard pagan productions that had far better have been left undone. For a while throughout Europe, Catholic art and traditions lay neglected and despised, while paganism ruled triumphantly in the palace, penetrated the cloister, and even raised its detested head under the vaulted cathedrals and over the high altars of Christendom. When these lamentable facts are considered, together with the fearful scourge in the form of war and revolution that has passed over the countries of the continent, involving abbey and cathedral, church and convent, in one common ruin, and reducing the most dignified clergy of France to the condition of stipendiary clerks, sharing a miserable pittance with the Calvinist minister and Jewish rabbi, received from the hands of a government official,—not one rood of land left for priest or altar, of all the vast estates which ancient piety had bequeathed,—we may find cause for thankfulness that matters are not worse than they are in our own country.

The spirit of Dunstan, of Anselm, and St. Thomas, were extinct ere that of Cranmer could have prevailed. We must not forget that this country was separated from the Holy See by the consent of the canonically instituted clergy of this realm, with a few noble but rare exceptions. The people were actually betrayed by their own lawful pastors. There were no missionaries from the Holy See to dispense the sacraments to those who remained faithful. And this vital change was effected without the least external demonstration: protestant opinions were not even broached till some years after the schism; the externals of religion remained precisely the same; and even when open scenes of sacrilege and violence began, they were conducted in some measure by authority: mass was sung by the old clergy in Canterbury, while the bones of its saintly martyr were burning in the garth, and his name and festival were erased by the churchmen from every missal and breviary in the country; while men of family and distinction, professing the old faith, and receiving the sacraments according to the ancient ritual, shared the property of the Church with avidity. And if we may judge from the disgraceful trials that have lately arisen, many who bear the name of Catholic would rob the Church in her present need and poverty, as eagerly and with as little remorse as they did in the days of her former possessions. I mention these things, because it is a common error, into which I was formerly led, to cast the whole odium of the loss of the ancient faith in England on the king and nobles, whereas the Catholic hierarchy of this land, who basely surrendered the sacred charge they should have defended even to death, essentially contributed to the sad change. It is true they never contemplated the possibility of such a state of things as we see, or, indeed, which shortly succeeded to their base compliance; and many who had weakly consented afterwards rallied, but too late. It is a true saying, " *C'est le premier pas qui coute ;*" and so indeed it turned out, to our bitter cost.

Regarding, therefore, the state of religion for the last three centuries as a punishment for the unfaithfulness of the English Church, we cannot but feel grateful that, notwithstanding all the repeated efforts and successes of the bitterest puritans, so many traces of the ancient paths have yet been preserved, to guide those who are now striving to regain the holy place. There is something surely providential in the retention of the ancient titles and dignities,—the daily chant of the divine office in the cathedrals and colleges,—the dedication of churches in honour of the ancient saints,—the consecration of ground for the burial of the dead,—the preservation of the chapel and order of England's patron, St. George,—the Catholic character of many portions of the liturgy, with its calendar of fasts and festivals,—the solemn service and anointing of the sovereign at the coronation. These, and many more, seem so many pledges that God will not be angry with this land for ever; for there is no other instance of a country having fallen into the miserable state of protestantism, having retained so much that is calculated to awaken in the breasts of her children a love and reverence for the past, and to lead them back to union with the see of blessed Peter, from whence the day-star of truth first beamed upon us.

Dugdale, Spelman, Bingham, Collier, Ashmole, and many illustrious English antiquaries and historians, might be cited to prove the great reverence for Catholic antiquity that was occasionally manifested in this

country, even while the puritan faction was proceeding to violence. The
spirit of Dugdale's text and plates is most Catholic; every line of his
Monasticon might have been written in a cloister of ancient Benedictines,
while his History of St. Paul's exhibits a depth of piety and devotion
towards the glory of God's Church, worthy of more ancient days.

Spelman, in his works, expresses himself on the subject of sacrilegious
spoliation in a manner that must strike shame and terror into the hearts
of those Catholics who would spoil the Church of which they profess
themselves the children; and he draws a fearful but true picture of the
dismal disasters that befel the plunderers of the Church at the period of
the general dissolution.

It is almost inconceivable that men, who had been educated in the
principles of the ancient faith, who had partaken of the sacraments
of the Church, and knelt at its altars, should have demolished, for the
sake of stone, timber, and lead, edifices whose beauty and skill would
have secured them from injury even in this generation, and which
should have possessed in their eyes the highest claim on their veneration; and we can only account for the atrocities which accom-
panied the ascendancy of protestantism in England, by supposing the
perpetrators blinded to the enormity of their own actions by the
punishment of God. To hear of the choirs of vast churches stript and
roofless,—tombs of prelates and nobles ransacked for lead,—brass rent
from graves,—the consecrated vessels of the sanctuary profaned and
melted,—the bones of saints and martyrs burnt,—the images of our
Divine Redeemer trodden under foot, dragged about and consumed,—
vestments converted to domestic use,—monastic libraries pillaged and
burnt,—and all this without foreign foe or invasion, in once and then
but lately Catholic England, and perpetrated by men who had been
born and bred in the Catholic Church,—seems like a fearful dream, and
almost incredible; and now the sad recital of destruction alone, moves
us more than even the record of ancient glory: we lament over the
prostrate pillars and scattered fragments of some once noble pile,—we

raise the fallen cross,—bare the ancient legend on the wall,—collect the fragments from the shattered panes, and clear the accumulating soil from moulded base and tomb. The study of Catholic antiquity is so associated with ancient piety and holy recollections, that the soul is insensibly drawn from the contemplation of material objects to spiritual truths.

An Englishman needs not controversial writings to lead him to the faith of his fathers; it is written on the wall, on the window, on the pavement, by the highway. Let him but look on the tombs of those who occupy the most honourable position in the history of his country, —the devout, the noble, the valiant, and the wise,—and he will behold them with clasped hands invoking the saints of Holy Church, whilst the legend round the slabs begs the prayers of the passers-by for their souls' repose. At Canterbury he beholds the pallium, emblem of the jurisdiction conferred by St. Gregory on the blessed Austen, first primate of this land; at York, the keys of Peter, with triple crowns, are carved on buttress, parapet, and wall. Scarcely one village church or crumbling ruin that does not bear some badge of ancient faith and glory. Now the crosses on the walls tell of anointings with holy chrism and solemn dedication,—the sculptured font, of sacraments seven, and regeneration in the laver of grace: the legend on the bell inspires veneration for these consecrated heralds of the Church; the chalice and host over priestly tomb teaches of altar and sacrifice; the iron-clasped ambry, sculptured in the wall, bears record of holy Eucharist reserved for ghostly food,—the stoups in porch, and Galilee of hallowed water, and purification before prayer; while window, niche, spandril, and tower set forth, by pious effigies, that glorious company of angels, prophets, apostles, martyrs, and confessors, who, glorified in heaven, watch over and intercede for the faithful upon earth.

The Cross—that emblem of a Christian's hopes—still surmounts spire and gable; in flaming red it waves from the masts of our navy, over the towers of the sovereign's palace, and is blazoned on London's shield.

H

The order of St. George, our patron saint, founded by King Edward of famous memory, is yet the highest honour that can be conferred by sovereigns on the subject; and his chapel is glorious, and his feast kept solemnly. Our cities, towns, and localities, the rocky islands which surround our shores, are yet designated by the names of those saints of old through whose lives, martyrdoms, or benefactions, they have become famous.

The various seasons of the year are distinguished by the *masses* of these holy tides. Scarcely is there one noble house or family whose honourable bearings are not identical with those blazoned on ancient church or window, or chantry tomb, which are so many witnesses of the pious deeds and faith of their noble ancestry. Nay, more, our sovereign is solemnly crowned before the shrine of the saintly Edward, exhorted to follow in the footsteps of that pious king, and anointed with oil poured from the same spoon that was held by Canterbury's prelates eight centuries ago.

In short, Catholicism is so interwoven with every thing sacred, honourable, or glorious in England, that three centuries of puritanism, indifference, and infidelity, have not been able effectually to separate it. It clings to this land, and developes itself from time to time, as the better feelings of a naturally honourable man who had been betrayed into sin. What! an Englishman and a protestant! Oh, worse than parricide, to sever those holy ties that bind him to the past, to deprive himself of that sweet communion of soul with those holy men, now blessed spirits with God, who brought this island from pagan obscurity to the brightness of Christian light,—who covered its once dreary face with the noblest monuments of piety and skill,—who gave those lands which yet educate our youth, support the learned, and from whom we received all we have yet left that is glorious, even to our political government and privileges.

Can a man of soul look on the cross-crowned spire, and listen to the chime of distant bells, or stand beneath the lofty vault of cathedral

+ CHVRCH FVRNITVRE REVIVED AT BIRMINGHAM

choir, or gaze on long and lessening aisles, or kneel by ancient tomb, and yet *protest* against aught but that monstrous and unnatural system that has mutilated their beauty and marred their fair design? Surely not. And truly such feelings of reverence for long-despised excellence has been awakened among so many of our learned and devout country-men, that we may begin to hope, indeed, that our redemption draws nigh. We have already lived to hear the name of Canterbury's blessed martyr pronounced with accents of veneration;—a hundred pens, most ably wielded, are writing in defence of ancient piety and practice;—a thousand voices are raised against the abominations of modern innovation. England is, indeed, awakening to a sense of her ancient dignity; she begins to appreciate the just merits of the past, and to work eagerly for the future. The last few years must, or ought to have, worked a great change in the feelings of English Catholics towards the Anglican church-men; and it is evident that, if it be God's will that departed glories are to be restored, it will be effected rather by rebuilding the ruined walls of Zion than by demolishing the poor remains that are left. The tide of popular innovation that so lately threatened us with common destruction seems providentially stayed. God forbid we should endeavour to obtain a transept in a scramble with dissenters, but rather prove ourselves to possess the feelings of the true mother in Solomon's judgment, and freely give up all, than see what we hold so dear divided; and by perfecting ourselves, and carrying out true Catholic principles in charity, devotion, and zeal, hasten forward that union to which, in the words of an eccle-siastical periodical, we may even begin to look forward, and which is rather to be obtained through the sacrifice of the altar and midnight supplication, than by the clamours of an election platform or the tumult of popular commotion.

Laus Deo!

DESCRIPTION

OF THE

REVIVED CHURCH ORNAMENTS FIGURED IN PLATE X.

In the centre, a lectern of carved oak, surmounted by a cross fleury, with a double desk turning on the shaft. A Psalter and book of the Holy Gospels, bound with clasps, and bosses of gilt metal, enamelled and engraved, are shown lying on it.

Immediately over the lectern is a corona or circlet for lights, and on either side an altar lamp.

On the altar are various examples of altar candlesticks, and a small tower tabernacle for the reservation of the blessed Eucharist.

The frontal represents the four Evangelists and other sacred emblems embroidered in needle-work and gold. On the step, two high standing candlesticks for consecration tapers.

Curtains suspended to rods are shown on each side of the altar; and, immediately behind the candlesticks and tabernacle, a small reredos of gilt or embroidered work, over which is a ferettum or portable shrine.

On the right side of the altar—

A processional cross.

A pastoral staff.

A faldistorium, with a precious mitre lying on it.

A monstrance.

Three chalices.

A standing altar cross.

On the left side of the altar—

A processional cross and a standing altar cross.

A pastoral staff.

A verge or cantor's staff.

A ciborium.

A pax and an Agnus Dei case.

On the pavement—

Two thuribles, with a ship for incense, two holy water vats, a processional candlestick, a chrismatory, enamelled, and a sacrying bell.

These ornaments, and many others, have been most faithfully revived from ancient authorities by the care of a devout and skilful goldsmith of Birmingham, and are produced by the ancient methods of working metals.

Lightning Source UK Ltd.
Milton Keynes UK
UKHW031927070820
367875UK00005B/187